Fruit

More Fruit

Much Fruit

Eugene A. Smith

Fruit

More Fruit

Much Fruit

Copyright © 2001 by Eugene A. Smith

Freedom Alive Ministries
www.freedomalive.ca

ISBN: 1-931178-95-X

Published by:

Vision Publishing
940 Montecito Way
Ramona, CA 92065

www.viu.com

To my friend, companion, and wife,
Darla,
who has sacrificed so much
for the sake of the
Gospel of Jesus Christ.

Acknowledgement

Without the cooperation of many people, this book
would never have become a reality.

I wish to thank my father-in-law,
Ray Brown,
for the many hours editing, proofing
and retyping of the manuscript.

Gratitude is also expressed to my wife, Darla Smith,
and my father, Colin Smith,
who helped proofing, editing and revising even further.

I must also recognize Dr. Stan DeKoven,
the president and founder of
Vision International University,
for reading my original manuscript, offering advice,
and encouraging me to put it into print.

Contents

Foreword

"Fruit – More Fruit – Much Fruit" is more than a survey of the fruit of the Spirit. It sets the study of the fruit mentioned in Gal. 5:22-23 in the larger context of the Holy Spirit's work in the process of salvation. The author also develops a fuller understanding of the fruit by showing the relationship between the work of the Holy Spirit and the return of Christ.

This book not only identifies the progressive work of the Holy Spirit to mold the believer into the image of Christ, but also further reveals how the fruit of the Spirit shapes the corporate Body of Christ.

In these days when God is working in many parts of the world, the teaching of the Holy Spirit as the unifying factor of the Body of Christ is most welcome. This work of the Holy Spirit is as much a demonstration of the supernatural power of God as are the gifts of the Spirit. The author does not try to cause the reader to choose between the fruit or the gifts, but shows how the work of the Holy Spirit is singular, and all His workings are to be embraced.

I first met Eugene while both he and I were in Africa teaching pastors' seminars and Bible school students. The message contained in this book is for all believers, regardless of where they live in the world. The lessons put forth here are applicable to the whole church worldwide.

I trust that you will be blessed as you read this study, with the result that you will be transformed into the image of Christ.

Dr. Stan DeKoven
Vision International University

Fruit ~ More Fruit ~ Much Fruit

The Fruit of the Spirit progresses from love toward God to love for others to self-control. The study of this progression is very rewarding and satisfying. The author sincerely desires that the readers of this work will not only see the beauty of the Fruit, but also be convinced of its necessity in our personal lives. Yet, it must proceed to the development of harmonious relationships among members of the Body of Christ. From eternity to eternity, the Father has planned to give His Son a Body through which He may express Himself, and the Fruit of the Spirit causes this to be a practical reality.

A note must be said about the words used in this book. The English language often changes word meanings. Words that had a specific meaning even a generation ago now carry a different connotation. This difficulty carries over into the many versions of the scriptures presently in use. A classic example may be the word "prevent" as found in 1 Thess. 4:15. In the older Authorized Kings James Version, the word means "to go before" while a modern reader may understand the word to mean "to stop." The modern understanding of the word "charity" has a different connotation than its use in the KJV. There charity means "love," but in today's use it means "to help the poor."

This same difficulty is encountered with such words as "longsuffering," "patience," "gentleness," "kindness," "faith," "meekness," "humility," and "temperance." The meanings and ideas that may come into the mind of one reader may not necessarily be the same as those of another. By drawing up a comparative list of the Fruit from various translations of scripture as outlined in Gal. 5:22-23, it is readily seen that the original Greek words are translated in a variety of ways. Sometimes the same English word is used to translate different Greek words! Note the following samples:

Greek	KJV	NKJV	NIV
Αγαπη	Love	Love	Love
Χαρα	Joy	Joy	Joy
Ειρηνη	Peace	Peace	Peace
Μακροθυμια	Longsuffering	Longsuffering	Patience
Χρηστοτης	Gentleness	Kindness	Kindness
Αγαθωσυνη	Goodness	Goodness	Goodness
Πιστις	Faith	Faithfulness	Faithfulness
Πραυτης	Meekness	Gentleness	Gentleness
Εγκρατεια	Temperance	Self-control	Self-control

Revised Standard	Good News	New American Bible	New American Standard
Love	Love	Love	Love
Joy	Joy	Joy	Joy
Peace	Peace	Peace	Peace
Patience	Patience	Patient endurance	Patience
Kindness	Kindness	Kindness	Kindness
Goodness	Goodness	Generosity	Goodness
Faithfulness	Faithfulness	Faith	Faithfulness
Gentleness	Humility	Mildness	Gentleness
Self-control	Self-control	Chastity	Self-control

To assist the reader, the author has chosen, when quoting scriptures throughout this book, to use the New King James Version (NKJV), but always to refer to the Fruit of the Spirit by name as written in the Authorized King James Version (KJV).

Great care has been taken to give definitions that are true to the original Greek words, based upon research and their usage throughout the New Testament. What has been sought after is the description of the character traits that were in Paul's mind when he penned the epistle to the Galatians.

May the Lord bless you as you embark upon this study! May He cause your life to be fruitful in every good work, causing you to blossom in love towards God, towards others, and control of self! May the Church shine forth and demonstrate the reality of the Body of Christ!

Eugene Smith

Chapter One

The Galatian Problem

Before we can appreciate the beauty of the fruit of the Spirit, we must understand the context of the Galatian problem. Then, we shall grasp the place the discussion of the fruit of the Spirit has in Paul's epistle to the Galatians.

Actually, the role of the Holy Spirit is central and crucial to Paul's argument throughout the epistle. Let us note the many verses in Galatians that refer to the Holy Spirit:

> *"This only I want to learn from you: Did you receive the **Spirit** by the works of the law, or by the hearing of faith? Are you so foolish? Having begun in the **Spirit**, are you now being made perfect by the flesh? Have you suffered so many things in vain – if indeed it was in vain? Therefore He who supplies the **Spirit** to you and works miracles among you, does He do it by the works of the law, or by the hearing of faith?" (Gal. 3:2-5)*

*"that the blessing of Abraham might come upon the Gentiles in Christ Jesus, that we might receive the promise of the **Spirit** through faith." (Gal. 3:14)*

*"And because you are sons, God has sent forth the **Spirit** of His Son into your hearts, crying out, 'Abba Father!' " (Gal. 4:6)*

*"But, as he who was born according to the flesh then persecuted him who was born according to the **Spirit**, even so it is now." (Gal. 4:29)*

*"For we through the **Spirit** eagerly wait for the hope of righteousness by faith." (Gal. 5:5)*

*"I say then: Walk in the **Spirit**, and you shall not fulfill the lust of the flesh. For the flesh lusts against the **Spirit**, and the **Spirit** against the flesh; and these are contrary to one another, so that you do not do the things that you wish. But if you are led by the **Spirit**, you are not under the law." (Gal. 5:16-18)*

*"But the fruit of the Spirit is **love, joy, peace, longsuffering, gentleness, goodness, faith, meekness, temperance**: against such there is no law." (Gal. 5:22-23 KJV)*

*"If we live in the **Spirit**, let us also walk in the **Spirit**." (Gal. 5:25)*

*"Brethren, if a man is overtaken in any trespass, you who are **spiritual** restore such a one in the spirit of gentleness, considering yourself lest you also be tempted. Bear one another's burdens, and so fulfill the law of Christ." (Gal. 6:1-2)*

*"For he who sows to the flesh will of the flesh reap corruption, but he who sows to the **Spirit** will of the **Spirit** reap everlasting life." (Gal. 6:8)*

Obviously, Paul intentionally provided many references to the Holy Spirit as he penned the epistle. Before we study these verses, we need to understand why Paul wrote Galatians, and the vital role the references to the Holy Spirit have in bringing doctrinal correction, and therefore truth, to the churches in Galatia.

It is obvious that Paul was very angry as he commenced his discussion concerning the situation in the churches. The great apostle was admonishing his readers, urging them to return to the gospel of Jesus Christ, which they were forsaking. In doing so, he confronted them very directly; there was no missing his opinion of their behaviour.

As was his custom in writing his epistles, Paul started this letter to the saints in Galatia by praying, *"Grace to you and peace from God the Father and our Lord Jesus Christ ..."* (Gal. 1:3-5). However, immediately after his prayer, he launched into the following tirade as he expressed his displeasure with the Galatians:

*"I marvel that you are turning away so soon from Him who called you in the grace of Christ, to a different gospel, which is not another; but there are some who trouble you and want to pervert the gospel of Christ. But even if we, or an angel from heaven, preach any other gospel to you than what we have preached to you, let him be accursed. As we have said before, so now I say again, **if anyone preaches any other gospel to you than what you have received, let him be accursed."** (Gal. 1:6-9)*

Undoubtedly, Paul was very agitated about a situation that had developed in the churches he had founded in the area. What could have caused him sufficient distress to generate such an outburst of emotion?

The Galatians were Gentile converts to Christianity. Paul had taught them that Gentile converts were as much the children of God as Jewish converts were. However, Paul always had to deal with people known as Judaizers who insisted that in order to be saved a person needed to be circumcised. They taught that a Gentile must be converted not only to Jesus but also to the Jewish faith.

After Paul left Galatia, the Judaizers travelled throughout the region, insisting that Gentiles who had believed on Christ through Paul's teaching become Jews and accept the "identity markers" of the Jewish faith, thus becoming genuine children of Abraham. They emphasized that in order to mature in Christ, these new converts had to observe the Jewish law. Therefore, in addition to circumcision (Gal. 5:2-3; 6:12), the Judaizers required the observance of the Jewish calendar (Gal. 4:10) and food laws (Gal. 2:11-14). Gentile converts were told that by becoming Jews they would receive the promises of God's covenant with Abraham:

*"I will bless those who bless you, And I will curse him who curses you; And in you **all the families of the earth shall be blessed.**" (Gen. 12:3)*

*"And the Lord said, 'Shall I hide from Abraham what I am doing, since Abraham shall surely become a great and mighty nation, and **all the nations of the earth shall be blessed in him?**' " (Gen. 18:17-18)*

The Judaizers did not contest the inclusion of Gentiles as members of the people of God; the initial element of faith did not seem to be disputed. They understood that, in God's covenant with Abraham, all families (nations) of the earth were to be blessed. *"And he (Abraham) believed in the Lord, and He accounted it to him for righteousness."* Gen. 15:6 was not unknown to the Judaizers. However, the basis on which the Gentiles could be accepted was bitterly contested.

Let's play the devil's advocate and take the part of one of those Judaizers who went into the region of Galatia after Paul had preached there. Miracles had taken place, and many had converted to Christ. After the Lord moved Paul out of the area, the teaching may have gone like this:

> God performed miracles through Paul, and some of you were healed; but God uses anybody. Paul taught you incorrect doctrine. You were saved by faith, and you received the Spirit. I am so happy for you, but let me show you where Paul is wrong. Aren't we told in the book of Genesis that Abraham was saved by faith? He believed God and it was counted to him for righteousness; yet, isn't it also true concerning Abraham, that after he believed God, circumcision was required? Therefore, you are saved by faith, but to grow as the people of God you must keep the Jewish laws. Abraham is our example. He believed God and he was circumcised later, as a sign. So Paul was confused. You need to be circumcised to be a child of God. Let me read from the Prophets to you:

> *"But this is the covenant that I will make with the house of Israel after those days, says the Lord: I will put My law in their minds, and write it on their hearts; and I will be their God, and **they shall be My people.**" (Jer. 31:33)*

In this new covenant, Jeremiah said that you would be
led into obedience to the law:

> *"I will give you a new heart and put a new spirit within
> you; I will take the heart of stone out of your flesh and
> give you a heart of flesh. I will put My Spirit within you
> and cause you to walk in My statutes, and **you will keep
> My judgments and do them."** (Ezek. 36:26-27)*

Ezekiel said that when you have received the Spirit,
which you Galatians have received, the Spirit would lead
you into obeying the law. You are saved by faith, but
you are matured and perfected by keeping the law.

The gospel that Paul preached stated that by faith in Christ Jesus
a person became a child of God. Only faith was required for
salvation. The Judaizers had introduced doctrinal error into the
gospel of Christ, and Paul, outraged at their activity, felt an ur-
gent need to make the necessary correction.

The dispute was not how a Gentile started the Christian life, but
rather how he progressed in and finished that life. By what principles must the life in Christ be lived? Does a Gentile Christian
live by faith in Christ or by keeping the Jewish law? Paul asked
the Galatians the following questions:

> *"O foolish Galatians! who has bewitched you that you
> should not obey the truth, before whose eyes Jesus Christ
> was clearly portrayed among you as crucified? This only
> I want to learn from you: Did you receive the Spirit by
> the works of the law, or by the hearing of faith? Are you
> so foolish?* **Having begun in the Spirit, are you now be-
> ing made perfect by the flesh?"** *(Gal. 3:1-3)*

Although the tone of Paul's voice may have sounded harsh to the Galatians, the words he spoke, full of great concern and compassion, should have betrayed his anger and touched their hearts. Paul was their spiritual father and could not tolerate the false doctrine being perpetrated among his spiritual children by the Judaizers.

In defending his gospel, and in refuting the doctrinal errors of those teachers of the law, Paul wrote a powerful exposition that centres around three points that are continually interwoven in the epistle. These three strands stand or fall together:

o   Righteousness is not by the works of the law.

o   Righteousness is by faith in Jesus Christ.

o   Christ by His Spirit lives in the believer.

Salvation does not come through the flesh or works of the law. None of us can say, that because I have kept all the precepts of God, I am counted righteous. Paul repeated this thought many times throughout the book of Galatians.

Due to the influence of the Reformation, the church of today can rightfully rejoice in the truth that justification is by faith alone, apart from works of the law. The foundation for Martin Luther's great revolution was built on the first two strands of Paul's discussion. However, this glorious truth contained in Paul's argument throughout the epistle, has tended to overshadow and somewhat colour the overall purpose of the book of Galatians. While justification by faith was certainly a central issue for Paul, it was not the end purpose for which the letter to the churches of Galatia was penned.

The third strand concerning the life of the Spirit is often over-looked when the study of Galatians is undertaken. The Judaiz-ers, attempting to persuade Paul's converts that he was teaching false doctrine, asked this question, **"What happens to right-eousness if the law is put away?"** If we do not lay down rules for people, what happens to righteousness? Paul argued that the Spirit living in the believer insures righteousness; the Spirit is the Spirit of righteousness. He replaces the law and produces a real righteousness, accomplishing what the law could never do. The Holy Spirit leads you into that which is right; He also con-victs you when you are wrong. The believer is to live by the Spirit, walk in the Spirit, and be led by the Spirit. The whole Christian life is the life of the Spirit. Without the gift of the Spirit, faith in Christ would be meaningless.

The gift of the Spirit proved to be the foundation upon which Paul built his response to the Judaizers' question. Indeed, life in the Spirit is a major focus of Paul's argument to defend his gos-pel of faith apart from the law. Failure to see this third point of Paul's discussion has led many to a rather disjointed reading of Galatians. The last part, especially from Gal. 5:13 to 6:10, is seen as some kind of addition and unrelated to the argument that has preceded it. This is common, but nothing could be further from the truth.

To understand Paul's many remarks about the Holy Spirit in this short epistle, it is important to comprehend the framework in which he understood the Spirit. The discussion concerning the Spirit in Galatians is in total agreement with the terms *"seal,"* *"guarantee (earnest),"* *"adoption,"* and *"firstfruits"* that Paul used elsewhere in scripture. All of these metaphors imply that the Holy Spirit is given to complete a process that has already begun.

Notice again in Galatians that the believer *"begins in the Spirit"* (3:3), *"waits through the Spirit for the hope of righteousness"* (5:5), and while waiting, he *"walks, is led by, lives in, and sows to the Spirit."* He prepares for the realization of that hope which the righteousness of the Spirit causes him to expect, and for which he waits (5:16, 18, 25; 6:8).

The initial act of believing on Christ (justification) is the inauguration of salvation. This takes care of guilt before the law. Salvation shall be consummated at Jesus' return (glorification). In the interim, salvation is a continuing process (sanctification).

Justification   **Sanctification**   **Glorification**
The "blessing of Abraham" becomes a reality from the 1ˢᵗ Coming of Christ until salvation's completion at the Lord's appearing.

Frequently, the term "the blessing of Abraham" has sonly referred to justification by faith and not to salvation from the beginning to the end. This view of salvation is much too limited and misses most of Paul's comments about the Holy Spirit. Paul makes the claim that the promise of the Spirit is the blessing of Abraham when he states in Gal. 3:14 *"that the blessing of Abraham might come upon the Gentiles in Christ Jesus, that we might receive the promise of the Spirit through faith."* The Holy Spirit is evidence of justification (Gal. 3:1-5; 4:6), the means for sanctification – for victory in this present life (Gal. 5:13-6:10), and for final glorification (Gal. 5:5). **The "blessing of Abraham" is the whole of salvation from beginning to end, from inauguration to consummation, from justification to glorification**. All three stages of salvation (justification, sanctification, glorification) are born by the Spirit, carried through by the Spirit, and completed by the Spirit. The beginning is simply an *"guarantee"* and a *"foretaste"* of the end. All of this, from being raised with Christ as a new creation to being raised physically at the last day, from being judged at the cross to the judgment of the last day, is included in the *"blessing of Abraham."* The "betrothal" will be absorbed into the "wedding."

The Spirit administers everything. Without Him, none of the promises included in God's covenant with Abraham could be made real in anyone's experience. Without the Spirit to actualize the covenant, there would be no adoption (Gal. 4:4-6; Rom. 8:15-17), washing, regeneration, or life (1 Cor. 6:11; Tit. 3:5; Rom. 8:2), sanctification (2 Thess. 2:13; 1 Pet. 1:2; 1 Cor. 6:11), or anointing (2 Cor. 1:21). Obviously, the Spirit is the crucial ingredient.

There is no doubt that Paul saw the gift of the Spirit in the same way the prophets did. The Holy Spirit is the agency through which God will cause all His promises, purposes, and goals to be realized (Isa. 32:15-17; 44:2-4; Ezek. 36:26-27; 37:14; 39:29). The promise of the Spirit spoken of by the prophets is none other than the "blessing of Abraham."

Thus the third strand of Paul's defence of his gospel becomes the driving force of his argument, without which the other two threads (justification not by works of the law and justification by faith in Christ Jesus) are left hanging and incomplete. Without the Holy Spirit, the other two truths are unshielded from criticism and without defence. For instance, if the third strand does not follow the other two, there is nothing to insure obedience and righteousness, thus defeating the very nature of salvation, which is to overturn sin, not to encourage it. The Spirit is the key element to faith and conversion, living in victory, and preparing the believer for the hope that lies ahead. Without Him, the entire scheme of salvation falls apart.

This overview will help us to see the fruit of the Spirit in focus. After Paul gave this list, he added: *"Against such there is no law."* (Gal. 5:22-23) When these virtues are evident in one's life, the law becomes irrelevant. There is no need to state, *"You shall not murder,"* when people love one another by the Spirit. Nor is the command, *"You shall not covet,"* necessary for those who actively pursue goodness out of kindness. The presence of the Holy Spirit, writing the righteousness of God upon the hearts of man, produces the real thing. The law was to "hem in" sin (Gal. 3:22). Now, the Spirit produces real righteousness. Thus, the fruit of the Spirit is the righteousness of God Himself reflected in His children.

Perhaps, all of this will take on even sharper distinction when we comprehend Paul's message of the cross. Not only Christ, but also the sinner is crucified. The gift of the Spirit is the resurrection side of the cross, and the new life is lived by the Spirit (Gal. 5:25). The message of the cross is the content of chapter two.

Thought Questions

1. Who were the Judaizers and what was their doctrine?

2. How would you describe Paul's attitude toward the Judaizers?

3. What are the three main arguments Paul puts forth in Galatians in defence of his gospel?

4. If submission to the law is put away, how is righteousness assured?

5. What is the blessing of Abraham?

6. Explain the whole scope of salvation – past, present, and future.

7. How does the fruit of the Spirit fulfill righteousness in the life of the believer?

Chapter Two

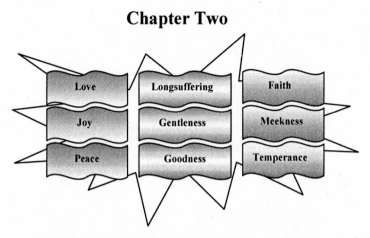

Love	Longsuffering	Faith
Joy	Gentleness	Meekness
Peace	Goodness	Temperance

The Preaching Of The Cross

*"O foolish Galatians! Who has bewitched you that you should not obey the truth, before whose eyes Jesus Christ was **clearly portrayed** among you as crucified?" (Gal. 3:1)*

The cross of Christ is central to Paul's gospel as preached to the Galatians. Indeed, this message delivered to the Gentile converts to Christ, produced a dynamic encounter with the Holy Spirit. Paul emphatically reminded the readers of this epistle that the truth concerning Christ crucified was very plainly made known to them. This truth was "clearly portrayed" among them.

"O foolish Galatians! Who has bewitched you...?" Paul inquired. Who has seduced you? Who has persuaded you not to obey the truth, but instead to return to keeping of the law – Sabbath days, feasts, and festivals? Why did Jesus die if works of law can make you righteous? When I preached the message of

the cross, the Holy Spirit made the gospel a vivid reality to you. It was as if you literally stood at the foot of the cross and watched Jesus die. Before your eyes, He was crucified for all to witness.

Can you hear the compassion, frustration and anger in Paul's voice as he reprimanded his beloved children in the faith? He could not tolerate their backsliding; he knew they must return to faith in Christ alone, forsaking all trust in the law.

> *"Paul, an apostle (not from men nor through man, but through Jesus Christ and God the Father who **raised Him from the dead**)," (Gal. 1:1)*

The first verse of the epistle clearly indicates that Paul intended to discuss the vital role the resurrection of Jesus Christ had in the gospel message. The death and resurrection of Christ included within it the death of the sinner, and the raising of the saint. God had assigned all of fallen humanity into Christ who, as the last Adam, was crucified:

> *"The first Adam became a living being. The last Adam became **a life-giving spirit.**" (1 Cor. 15:45)*

> *"For the love of Christ compels us, because we judge thus: that **if One died for all, then all died**; and He died for all, that those who live should live no longer for themselves, but for Him who died for them and rose again." (2 Cor. 5:14, 15)*

> *"Therefore, if anyone is in Christ, **he is a new creation**; old things have passed away; behold, all things have become new." (2 Cor. 5:17)*

*"For in Christ Jesus neither circumcision nor uncircum-
cision avails anything, but **a new creation**." (Gal. 6:15)*

Therefore, all of fallen humanity was crucified in Christ, and
every follower of Christ is raised a new creation.

This concept of identification with Christ in death and in resurrection is one of the foundations throughout Paul's argument.
Consequently, it needs elaboration. There are several references
to this truth as noted in the following verses:

*"For I through the law **died** to the law that I might **live**
to God. I have been **crucified with Christ**; it is no longer
I who live, but Christ lives in me; and the life which I
now live in the flesh I live by faith in the Son of God, who
loved me and gave Himself for me." (Gal. 2:19, 20)*

Paul says that the law condemned us as sinners. Before the law
we were found guilty, and the law executed us at the cross with
Christ. We deserved to die; we did die, and now we live different lives - lives lived to God:

*"For as many of you as were **baptized into Christ have
put on Christ**." (Gal. 3:27)*

Baptized into Christ means that we were identified with His
death and His resurrection:

*"And those who are Christ's **have crucified the flesh**
with its passions and desires. If we **live in the Spirit**, let
us also walk in the Spirit." (Gal. 5:24, 25)*

"Live in the Spirit" is equivalent to "raised with Christ."

*"But God forbid that I should boast except in the cross
of our Lord Jesus Christ, by whom **the world has been
crucified to me, and I to the world.**" (Gal. 6:14)*

How are we set free from the power of the world? We have been
crucified to the world. The world has no power to influence a
crucified (dead) person. Just as a dead alcoholic cannot be
tempted by alcohol, a crucified person cannot be tempted by the
world.

Paul had warned the Galatians, when he first preached the gospel to them, that God had condemned the practices of the heathen. Any who practice such deeds, now described as the "works
of the flesh," would not inherit the kingdom of God (5:19-21).
Man is flesh and therefore enslaved to such works. The salvation
story must bring an effectual end to the reign and tyranny of the
flesh:

*"But now we have been delivered from the law, having
died to what we were held by, so that **we should serve in
the newness of the Spirit** and not in the oldness of the
letter." (Rom. 7:6)*

*"For I know that in me (that is, in my **flesh**) nothing
good dwells; for to will is present with me, but how to
perform what is good I do not find." (Rom. 7:18)*

*"For I delight in the law of God according to the **inward
man**." (Rom. 7:22)* {The expressions "inward man" and
"inner man" are synonymous.}

As Paul described life in the Spirit in penning his letter to the
Romans, he employed the words "spirit," "inner man," and
"flesh." These terms are preferred to the more common words

"spirit," "soul," and "body" used in 1 Thess. 5:23. The spirit is
to be the center of man's being, and is to be filled by the life of
God Himself. The inner man is simply a reference to an individual's character makeup. One person may be more emotional
than others, while another may be stimulated intellectually. Another may be more strong-willed. Finally, at this point and before the term undergoes an expansion of meaning, flesh refers to
the physical body that relates to this earth. At the original creation, God pronounced all, including the flesh (physical body), as
"very good" (Gen. 1:31).

The order of the original creation may be viewed as follows:

SPIRIT **INNER MAN** **FLESH**	In the original creation of man, pronounced very good by the Lord, the spirit was to be the controlling factor. Communication with the Lord was to take place in the spirit. All of life's development would result from dependence on, and relationship with, the Lord. Thus the inner man would take form and be expressed as a consequence of that relationship. The flesh (body) would then be the vehicle of expression upon the earth.

In this condition, man was to be fully dependent upon God as
the source of all life and knowledge. Satan tempted man, who

was made in God's image, by suggesting that he could live independently from God, making his own decisions regarding good and evil. No longer would God need to be the source of all things. In effect, man would be like God (Gen. 3:5)!

Satan lied. Though each person, after the fall in the Garden of Eden, would determine for himself his own standard of good and evil, man did not become a god in the sense of being like his creator. Rather, the fallen man became a slave to his own flesh. Because of disobedience, the original order changed. No longer would the spirit be predominant. As warned (Gen. 3:3), man did "die" when he ate the forbidden fruit of the tree of the knowledge of good and evil. Fallen man may be viewed as follows:

| **SPIRIT WITHOUT LIFE**

FLESH

INNER MAN | In the fallen state, the spirit of man does not relate to God. Relationship and communication are no longer a way of life. Without the Spirit's influence, the flesh is the predominate factor, enslaving the inner man. Paul refers to this order as either the "old man" (Rom. 6:6) or the "flesh." This is the state of every person who is not "born again" and describes man outside Christ. It refers to man as he relates to this present world that has been judged and is passing away. |

Man left in this state was dangerous to himself and society. Because the flesh now dominated the inner man, controls became necessary to keep him from fulfilling his evil desires. What was there to stop a man from committing murder, theft, or adultery? How could society be preserved? What would keep the nation of Israel intact until something could be done to reverse the awful effects of the fall?

To deal with this situation, God gave the law. One of the purposes of the law was to restrain the expression of sin:

> *"But the Scripture has confined all under sin, that the promise by faith in Jesus Christ might be given to those who believe. But before faith came, **we were kept under guard by the law**, kept for the faith which would afterward be revealed." (Gal. 3: 22-23)*

The law could not deal with anger in the heart, but it could, by means of threat and punishment, keep a person from expressing that anger. The Pharisees of Jesus' day completely misunderstood the entire intent and purpose of the law. They thought that outward obedience to the law made them "holy." Jesus did not agree with their interpretation (Matt. 5). The Lord taught that sin has its source in the heart, and righteousness is definitely a matter of the heart. Though the law could keep a person from committing murder by means of threat and punishment, it could do nothing about the anger itself. Therefore the law was given to "imprison" man, to "enslave" him, so that he could not do the things that he really wanted to do:

> *"For the flesh lusts against the Spirit, and the Spirit against the flesh; and these are contrary one to another, so that **you do not do the things that you wish**." (Gal. 5:17)*

The "jail-house" was needed until the time would come that something could be done with the heart itself. If there were an effective method of dealing with the flesh and setting the inner man free, then there would no longer be a need for this slavery to which the law subjects man. The cross of Christ and the gift of the Spirit are God's response to the problem of the flesh.

However, in this time of enslavement by the law, man may be viewed as follows:

THE LAW **FLESH** **INNER MAN**	Nothing has changed from before, except that the restraint of the law is imposed upon fallen man. The dominance of the flesh is not broken, and the inner man is still bound by its power. The law has no power to justify, deliver, or make righteous. Therefore, it had a temporary role until the time would come when a more efficient manner of dealing with the issue of fallen man would appear. Then there would be no further use for the "jail-house."

The "more efficient manner" is the cross of Christ. However, it is not just the death of the Savior, but as Paul states many times in Galatians, **it is the death of the sinner included in the death**

of Christ. When all the prisoners have been executed, obviously there is no more need for the jail. The law has performed its function and is no longer needed.

The Scripture teaches that the Son of God robed Himself in flesh. This is referred to as the "incarnation" (Heb. 2:14; Phil. 2:7; John 1:14). To put sin to death was one of the reasons for Christ being made in the likeness of sinful flesh. When Christ hung on the cross, it was flesh that was being crucified. Christ was the only person who had never violated the law in any aspect, yet he voluntarily suffered the wrath of the law upon the cross. Being without blemish, He was the only one qualified to make atonement for sin. He offered himself, was crucified in the flesh, and then was raised from the dead.

What does it mean to believe in Christ? Christ was our substitute. He did for man what man could not do. However, the gospel states that not only Christ died, but also the sinner was taken to death with Him. To believe in Christ is not just to give a "mental assent" which quickly degenerates into "easy believism." It is to believe into Christ, that is, to become a participant in His death and resurrection. It is not just an acceptance of historical fact, but involvement with those facts.

In other words, the preaching of the gospel invites sinners to share in the death and resurrection of Christ. The "old man" or "flesh" is guilty of many crimes, and thus is worthy of death. By believing into Christ, this death sentence is executed. All charges are satisfied, and no other charges can ever be laid. Death is the end of it all.

The other side of believing into Christ is the resurrection. Indeed, by death old things have passed away, and now by resurrection all things have really become new (2 Cor. 5:17). A *"new man"* comes into view (Eph. 4:24). Christ indwells the believer by the Holy Spirit. The powerful gift of the Holy Spirit is the resurrection life. The "new man" may be viewed as follows:

| SPIRIT FILLED WITH THE HOLY SPIRIT INNER MAN   FLESH | The cross and the gift of the Holy Spirit are God's response to the problem of the flesh. The "old man," in whom the flesh dominated, has been removed by death. The inner man is set free. The Holy Spirit does what the law could never do. It restores man to a better state than the original creation. God Himself, in the person of the Holy Spirit, takes up residence within man. **He insures righteousness by giving him a new heart, and by writing His own laws upon that new heart. These laws are the life of Christ Himself.** Now, He imparts His desires as a new instinctive behavior reflecting the true righteousness. This is the law of Christ: *"Bear one another's burdens, and so fulfill the law of Christ."* (Gal. 6:2) |

The role of the Spirit must not be underestimated. It is central to Paul's discussion throughout Galatians. He argued that the gift of the Spirit fulfilled the promise of Abraham (Gal. 3:14). He agreed with all the prophets that the promises of God were made functional and realized through the agency of the Holy Spirit (c.f. Ezek. 36:26, 27).

The gift of the Spirit is proof of sonship (Gal 4:6). By the same Spirit, believers wait for the *"hope of righteousness"* (Gal. 5:5), which is none other than the Lord's appearing, at which time believers will be glorified together with Him (Col. 3:4). This glorification is the ultimate expression of the work of the Spirit in the believer, transforming even his physical body into one that is suited for eternity, a *"spiritual body"* (1 Cor. 15:44). This body will be free from weakness and fatigue. It will be in perfect harmony with the Spirit, executing the Spirit's desires without restrictions or objections.

By believing into Christ, one begins life in the Spirit. Just as the term *"in the flesh"* refers to the old man outside Christ, now the term *"in the Spirit"* refers to the new creation. The ultimate state of the believer is to be fully transformed by the Spirit at the coming of the Lord. For now, believers have *"begun in the Spirit"* (Gal. 3:3), but life in the Spirit is not automatic. While waiting to be completed in that day, believers must *"walk in the Spirit"* (Gal. 5:16), *"be led by the Spirit"* (Gal. 5:18), *"live in the Spirit"* (Gal. 5:25), and *"sow to the Spirit"* (Gal. 6:8). Thus, the *"fruit of the Spirit"* (Gal. 5:22-23) will be formed, and they will be ready for the final expression of the Spirit: **glorification with Christ! Hallelujah!**

Thought Questions

1. Which of the following statements is the more accurate description: (a) I received the benefits of the death, burial, and resurrection of Christ or (b) I participate in the death, burial, and resurrection of Christ?

2. A quick reading of the book of Acts reveals that water baptism occurred immediately after conversion. What do you think is the reason for this?

3. What is the connection between being raised with Christ and the gift of the Spirit?

4. Are you able to describe salvation in terms of the effect on the spirit, inner man, and flesh?

5. What role did the law take in the process of salvation?

6. How does the Holy Spirit replace the law?

7. What is the importance of living after the Spirit?

Chapter Three

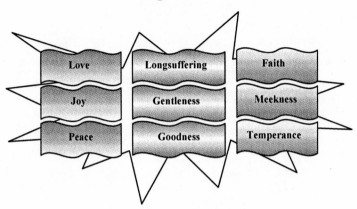

Fruit And Gifts

Unfortunately, many believers have chosen either the gifts of the Spirit or the fruit of the Spirit. However, scripture does not offer us this option. The believer is to be filled with the Spirit, who produces both gifts and fruit. There is only one Spirit, and His work is not divided. The same Holy Spirit who grants miraculous gifts of healings also prompts the vessels He uses to put away bitterness.

The work of the Holy Spirit is to reveal Christ. This He does by producing the nature and character of Christ within, and empowering for service outwardly. In other words, the same Holy Spirit produces fruit and gives gifts:

> *"My little children, for whom I labor in birth again until* ***Christ be formed in you,"*** *(Gal. 4:19)*

> *"But when it pleased God, who separated me from my mother's womb and called me through His grace, to reveal His Son **in me**, that I might preach Him among the*

Gentiles, I did not immediately confer with flesh and blood," (Gal. 1:15-16)

*"But we all, with unveiled face, beholding as in a mirror the glory of the Lord, **are being transformed into the same image** from glory to glory, just as by the Spirit of the Lord." (2 Cor. 3:18)*

*"There are diversities of gifts, but the same Spirit. There are differences of ministries, but the same Lord. And there are diversities of activities, but it is the same God who works all in all. But the manifestation of the Spirit is given to each one for the profit of all: for to one is given the **word of wisdom** through the Spirit, to another the **word of knowledge** through the same Spirit, to another **faith** by the same Spirit, to another **gifts of healings** by the same Spirit, to another the **working of miracles**, to another **prophecy**, to another **discerning of spirits**, to another **different kinds of tongues**, to another the **interpretation of tongues**. But one and the same Spirit works all these things, distributing to each one individually as He wills." (1 Cor. 12:4-11)*

Although scripture offers no option to choose between fruit and gifts, it **commands** us to embrace all the Holy Spirit desires to accomplish. We are admonished to *"pursue love, **and** desire spiritual gifts"* (1 Cor. 14:1). However, there seem to be two extremes. One the one hand, there are those who deny any of the miraculous ability of the Holy Spirit, suggesting that all that belongs to an age past, and is not applicable today. The emphasis in their preaching is living righteously and having strong homes. These are excellent and scriptural goals. On the other hand, there are those that are enthralled with the outwardly visible miraculous side of the Holy Spirit, and place all their emphasis on this to the exclusion of anything else He wishes to achieve in their lives. They speak in tongues, but they have dysfunctional homes. Humility is lacking, and relationships with others are difficult.

Neither approach to righteous living is correct. We are to embrace the work of the Holy Spirit in all that He does. We need godly lives, demonstrating love one for another so that all men will know that we are Christ's disciples (Jn. 13:34-35), but we also need the power to deliver the oppressed from bondage.

A very common illustration showing the need for both fruit and gifts is taken from the Old Testament. The robe that Aaron the High Priest wore in the service of the sanctuary is described in Ex. 28:31-35. The hem was decorated with both golden bells and colored pomegranates. They alternated around the hem of his garment. Many expositors of scripture interpret this arrangement as illustrative of the need for harmonious working together of fruit and gifts. If the fruit were not there, the bells would have clashed continuously. Paul possibly had this illustration in mind when he wrote 1 Cor. 13:1: *"Though I speak with the tongues of men and of angels, **but have not love**, I have become sounding brass or a clanging cymbal."* The presence of spiritual gifts outside the context of love should be avoided.

Love for others will often be expressed through the gifts of the Spirit. As we follow love, we will unconsciously find ourselves praying for others. Love prompts us to reach out to the Lord for the salvation and healing of everyone. Love demands that we cast out demons, and speak an encouraging prophetic word to those in need. The gifts of the Spirit become the vehicle by which love is practically ministered to a sin-sick world. Others are lifted up when these wonderful gifts function in the body of Christ.

The story of Moses is replete with interesting illustrations of life's victories, shortcomings and difficulties. Early in his life, both fruit and gifts were lacking. In his own strength and wisdom, he slew an Egyptian (Ex. 2:11-15), as if deliverance would come by his hands (Acts. 7:22-29).

He fled Egypt and spent many years on the backside of the desert. The harsh conditions of desert living were instrumental in delivering him from pride and self-reliance. When God spoke to him from the burning bush, Moses did not readily accept the call on his life; he permitted fear and intimidation to rule his thoughts. Moses attempted to persuade God that he was not the man for the job. Inward grace had been wrought in his character, but he lacked power (Ex. 3:1-11). To accomplish the task ahead of him, gifts had to be added. God gave him supernatural signs: his rod turned into a serpent and back into a rod again; his hand became leprous and normal again; and water changed into blood (Ex. 4:1-9).

The task of evangelizing the world and building the church requires the supernatural ability and power of God, not our power, strength, and wisdom.

Another incident in his life provided evidence that Moses required the "sandpaper" treatment to smooth an undesirable facet of his character. The Lord had supplied the personnel – the children of Israel – to accomplish the task.

The people had complained to Moses about the poor conditions in which they found themselves. Moses' patience was severely tested, and even though he sought the Lord and received his instructions, Moses struck the rock in anger, hitting it twice (Num. 20:2-13). However, the miracle still occurred. Water flowed from the rock in great abundance, sufficient for the entire congregation and all their animals. Though the miracle happened, Moses had misrepresented God's character. Moses, who at times seemed prone to impatience with the people and their complaints (c.f. Num. 11:11-15), wrongly projected his impatience onto God, and led the people to believe that God was angry with them. In reality, God would rather have mercy than bring judgment. In spite of the nation's shortcomings, God still loved them and provided for them.

The following event in Moses' life shows the beauty of both fruit and gifts. Moses was on the mountain communing with God. The people below had made a golden calf and were committing spiritual idolatry. See how beautifully Moses interceded on their behalf, but how strong he was in outward authority as he executed the offenders (Ex. 32:11-35). During this incident, Moses shone in both inward graces and outward power. This is the correct way to embrace the Holy Spirit. We are to know both His character and His power. Neither one is optional. The same Holy Spirit produces both, and His work is singular.

The perspective that Paul gives in 1 Cor. 13 needs to be heard again. Love is eternal, and will not pass away when the world does. What is in a man's heart will be taken into eternity. The gifts of the Spirit as they are known now will not be needed in eternity, and therefore are temporal, belonging to this age only. For instance, gifts of healings will not be needed for resurrected bodies! Workings of miracles will not be required when everything is in perfect harmony with the Spirit. The gifts of the Spirit are a foretaste of the powers of the world to come, and are simply how the Holy Spirit manifests Himself while sin is still a present reality. When the presence of sin is removed at the resurrection, these manifestations of the Holy Spirit will cease, and we will know the perfect fullness of the Spirit totally outside the context of a sinful environment. We shall discover in that day that love, the sum of all the fruit, is eternal. Indeed, love is the nature of God Himself.

A strong warning needs to be sounded concerning the fallacy of pursuing spiritual gifts outside the context of love. While fruit is the development of Christ-like character and the result of growth, the gifts are "on loan." They are given by God and are not earned. The Greek word for gift here is "charisma" which is the word "charis" followed by the suffix "ma." Charis means "grace" and the suffix means "a portion of." Spiritual gifts are portions of grace for use by the believer. They are called spiritual gifts, not because the believer is "spiritual," but because they come from the Holy Spirit. That should be obvious from the scripture, but many people seem to miss this simple point. Mere babes in Christ, new converts can speak in tongues and prophesy (Acts. 19:1-6). Therefore the presence and operation of spiritual gifts are not proofs of spirituality, but the grace of God.

The Corinthian church was a prime example of the pursuit of spiritual gifts outside the context of love. The grace of God was abundantly extended toward them, and they were enriched in all utterance and knowledge. They came behind in no gift (1 Cor. 1:4-9). This thoroughly carnal church was in danger of being destroyed (1 Cor. 3:1-4, 16-17).

Some very strong warnings are given us in scripture concerning this problem. A person who pursues sensation or outward power without submitting to the work of the Holy Spirit in the heart is already deceived, and is a candidate for further deception. Consider the solemn warnings from the lives of Balaam, Samson, King Saul, and Judas Iscariot.

Although some of Balaam's prophetic words are of the utmost beauty, he was covetous (Jude 11; 2 Pet. 2:15-16). Balak, king of the Moabites, feared Israel because of what they had done to the Amorites. He offered to pay Balaam if he would speak a curse over Israel. God instructed Balaam not to go with Balak's emissaries, for Israel was blessed. Balak then sent more dignitaries of higher rank and honor with a promise of an even greater reward for Balaam. Even though Balaam had already heard God on this matter, he sought the Lord again. He was determined to find a way to collect the reward money. God this time permitted him to go, though He had previously said no. As Balaam went to deliver a curse on Israel, his life was spared only because his donkey saw an angel with a drawn sword!

Obviously, Balaam's motive was completely wrong, and this incident provided a strong warning to him. Instead of cursing Israel, Balaam blessed it several times, but solicited God first each time. Balaam was dismayed.

Ultimately, Balaam thought of a way to collect the reward money. God had not allowed him to curse Israel, but he told Balak how to cause Israel to bring a curse upon itself. He counseled Balak to send in Moabite women to tempt them to commit whoredom. This would bring the anger of the Lord into their midst, and they would be destroyed from within. Balak followed this counsel with a measure of success. Only the quick action of Moses diverted the fierce anger of God in this matter (Num.22-25).

Later, when the Midianites were conquered, Balaam was slain along with them (Num. 31:8, 16). At the end of his life, Balaam was not recognized as a prophet, but as a soothsayer (Josh. 13.22). **Indeed, it is dangerous not to seek the fruit of the Spirit while pursuing the sensational.**

Samson's story is told in Judges 13-16. He was anointed of God
for power, but he willfully sinned continuously. He could powerfully rip the gates of the city off the wall and walk away with
them right after he spent the night with a harlot. It is obvious
that the gifts of God are not merited, and their presence does not
testify to the spirituality of the individual, or the correctness of
the doctrine that shaped the lifestyle.

Samson's involvement with Delilah eventually cost him his life,
but the anointing and call of God upon his life did not altogether
leave him. When his hair grew back, he brought down the temple, killing the Philistines and himself in the process.

In the beginning, Saul was anointed and even prophesied along
with the prophets (1 Sam. 10:6, 10). By the power of the anointing he was "turned into another man" and led the nation into
military victories. King Saul would not deal with jealousy in his
heart toward David (1 Sam. 18:9). His character was unstable,
and pride had set in. On more than one occasion, Saul would not
listen to Samuel, and was finally rejected by God as king. He
was not teachable and he was unwilling to deal with the anger
and envy that plagued his life. These character flaws were his
downfall. Eventually the Spirit of the Lord left him, and an evil
spirit from the Lord troubled him (1 Sam. 16:14). Nevertheless,
even in this condition, Saul could still prophesy when he encountered the Spirit of God at Ramah (1 Sam. 19:19-24). However, he would prophesy with bizarre manifestations, stripping
himself as he prophesied. This was the result of a clash between
the Holy Spirit and the evil spirit.

It is obvious from this extreme example that the sensational is
no guarantee of truth, and though God by His grace pours out
gifts, gifts are not the indicator of correctness in a person's life
or in the life of a congregation. What is disturbing in Saul's case

is that the demonic continued to use him in the prophetic after the Spirit of the Lord had left him (1 Sam. 18:10).

Judas Iscariot is another example that should serve as a warning. With the rest of the disciples, Judas received charismatic ability with power to heal the sick and cast out demons (Matt. 10:1-8; Acts 1:16-17; Mark 6:7; Luke 9:1-6). Yet during this time, he harbored wrong thoughts and expectations. In the end, he would not be submissive to the teaching of Jesus. He was disappointed with Jesus for refusing the offer of the five thousand to make him king of Israel. This allowed apostasy to develop in his heart, opening the door for Satan to enter (John 6:1-71, esp. vv. 66-71; 13:27).

Jesus made the issue crystal clear in the Sermon on the Mount:

> *"Be aware of false prophets, who come to you in sheep's clothing, but inwardly are ravenous wolves. You will know them by their fruits. Do men gather grapes from thornbushes or figs from thistles? Even so, every good tree bears good fruit, but a bad tree bears bad fruit. A good tree cannot bear bad fruit, nor can a bad tree bear good fruit. Every tree that does not bear good fruit is cut down and thrown into the fire. Therefore by their fruit you will know them. **Not everyone who says to Me, 'Lord, Lord,' shall enter the kingdom of heaven, but he who does the will of My Father in heaven.** Many will say to Me in that day, 'Lord, Lord, have we not prophesied in Your name, cast out demons in Your name, and done many wonders in Your name?' And then I will declare to them, 'I never knew you; depart from Me, you who practice lawlessness!' " (Matt. 7:15-23)*

These examples should convince everyone that charismatic ability is not the measuring stick of spirituality. The scripture makes it abundantly clear, however, that the fruit of the Spirit is! Any person or congregation that boasts of gifts but does not pursue fruit will be destroyed. Without the fruit, the gifts inevitably lead to arrogance. With the fruit, the gifts become mighty expressions of the love of God to a lost and dying world.

Thought Questions

1. Why do you think many believers tend to choose be-tween fruit and gifts instead of embracing the whole ac-tivity of the Holy Spirit?

2. In 1 Corinthians 13:1-3, how does Paul describe the gifts of the Spirit without the corresponding fruit of the Spirit?

3. This chapter identified various phases from the life of Moses: excelling in power; shining forth in character; and demonstrating both fruit and giftings. Identify such incidents from your own life.

4. Balaam, Samson, King Saul, and Judas Iscariot all ex-perienced the supernatural gifts of the Spirit. Should they be considered spiritual people?

5. State in your own words what true spirituality means.

Chapter Four

Fruit

Faith, Hope, and Love

In the Garden of Eden, two trees stood out from the others. One was the *"tree of life"* and the other was the *"tree of the knowledge of good and evil."* The tree of life represents God's life, the life of the Spirit. It leads to dependence upon God for all things. The tree of the knowledge of good and evil represents independence, reliance upon one's self instead of God.

When Adam ate fruit from the tree of the knowledge of good and evil, man became filled with himself, rather than filled with God. Unfortunately, the flesh became the predominant factor in his life and robbed him of his true powers and capabilities.

The difference between the two lifestyles is enormous. Life in the Spirit is one of fruit (Gal 5:22); life in the flesh is one of works (Gal. 5:19). The former is one of resting and abiding, while the latter is full of striving, exertion and labor. One lifestyle is divine empowerment; the other is human endeavor. As we feed on Christ, choosing the way of the tree of life, the fruit of the Spirit is evidenced in our lives, reflecting the righteousness of God.

Let us note this reference to the fruit of the Spirit:

> *"For all the law is fulfilled in one word, even this: 'You shall **love** your neighbor as yourself.' " (Gal. 5:14)*

The first fruit of the Spirit is love. According to the above scripture, love fulfills all the requirements of the law. Love is the greatest of the virtues. If you love your neighbor, do you need to be told not to kill him, not to covet his possessions, and not to steal his property? If the Holy Spirit causes the love of God to be shed abroad in your hearts, and you keep the one commandment to love your neighbor, then the righteousness of the law will be fulfilled in you. You will be keeping the Ten Commandments because of love, rather than as a result of the pressure of the law. What a difference there is! The way of love is fruit; the way of force is works.

At this point in our discussion, it will be advantageous for us to consider Paul's famous triad: faith, hope, and love.

> *"For we through the Spirit eagerly wait for the **hope** of righteousness by **faith**. For in Christ Jesus neither circumcision nor uncircumcision avails anything, but faith working through **love**." (Gal. 5:5-6)*

This is one of many times Paul uses this triad together in the scriptures. The most common one is found in 1 Cor. 13:13:

> *"And now abide **faith**, **hope**, **love**, these three; but the **greatest of these is love**."*

We are going to discover that the fruit of the Spirit is simply manifestations of love. It is the one fruit "love" manifesting various aspects of its nature such as gentleness, meekness and goodness. The fruit of the Spirit is simply the progressive development of the virtue love.

A definition for each of these terms is necessary. In Galatians 5:5, Paul says we wait for the hope of righteousness. This correctly places hope in the future, agreeing with Romans 8:24-25:

"For we were saved in this hope, but hope that is seen is not hope; for why does one hope for what he sees? But if **we hope for what we do not see**, *we eagerly wait for it with perseverance."*

Hope is the fulfillment of a word from God, but the fulfillment has not yet taken place. It is sure and guaranteed, but not possessed yet. For instance, scripture refers to the *"blessed hope:"*

"looking for the **blessed hope** *and* **glorious appearing of our great God and Savior Jesus Christ**, *who gave Himself for us, that He might redeem us from every lawless deed and purify for Himself His own special people, zealous for good works." (Tit. 2:13-14)*

What a blessed hope we have! His appearing will be glorious and include such momentous events as the resurrection of the body, the kingdom to come, crowns, rewards, and other related events that all belong to the believer's hope.

Since all these things are true, but not yet manifested in time, the word "hope" has a secondary use in scripture. It means to have the mind garrisoned with a positive, cheery attitude. Since the end is guaranteed, our outlook in the present should always be bright, irrespective of our present circumstances. The world does not know this meaning of hope, and tends to use the word to express a desire that has no guarantee associated with it.

How do we wait for the fulfillment of God's promise? We wait by faith. According to Hebrews 11:1, *"Now faith is the substance of things hoped for, the evidence of things not seen."* Faith is an inner convictive persuasion that knows God will do as He said. Faith directs a person to live according to what God has spoken, even if it has not been fulfilled yet! It lives in anticipation of the promised end.

Recall Joseph's two dreams as told in Genesis:

> *"There we were, binding sheaves in the field. Then, behold, my sheaf arose and also stood upright; and indeed* **your sheaves stood all around and bowed down to my sheaf.***"(Gen. 37:7)*

> *"...Look, I have dreamed another dream. And this time, the* **sun, the moon, and the eleven stars bowed down to me.***"(Gen. 37:9)*

Joseph was seventeen years old when God gave him these two dreams; he was thirty-nine when his eleven brothers bowed down before him in Egypt. Twenty-two years had passed from the time of his receiving the dreams until their complete fulfillment occurred.

Joseph believed that God had spoken to him through the dreams, placing a call on his life. He had maintained that belief despite his brothers' betrayal, sending him to Egypt as a slave. In spite of the facts concerning Potiphar's wife, his lengthy jail sentence, and the butler's forgetting about him, Joseph preserved God's word to him through many years because of his inner persuasion that the outcome would be as God had said. Does this portion of Joseph's life interpret for you the meaning of *"faith is the substance of things hoped for, the evidence of things not seen"*?

Faith will be challenged by present circumstances. The believer must choose to follow either the word of the Lord, or what his natural senses dictate. Many challenges will arise between the time God speaks a word, and the fulfillment of that word. We are to respond to these challenges with faith. This standing the test of faith will produce a character change (1 Pet. 1:6-9; Heb. 10:39). When doubts, fears, and discouragements are overcome by adhering to what God has spoken, a reformation takes place in the soul. This is what is meant when Paul said, *"faith works by love."* Faith causes our lives to go through character change, and the end to which God is leading is love. Faith gives birth to love, and then expresses itself through that love. This love is none other than the fruit of the Spirit.

If Joseph's word of the Lord had been fulfilled two months after he heard it, perhaps he would have killed his brothers. He would have taken revenge by using his authority to destroy them. However, the great plans God had for Joseph included major character modifications before he could become prime minister of Egypt. Consequently, God allowed his faith to be continuously challenged. Finally, after many faith victories and the associated character changes, Joseph was ready to inherit the word of the Lord:

> *"But we are not of those who draw back to perdition, but of those **who believe to the saving of the soul**." (Heb. 10:39)*

Joseph was one of those who believed to the saving of his soul. His faith stood the test of time, bringing a marvelous reformation of character into his life. He now had the capacity to love those who had perpetrated evil deeds against him:

> *"And Joseph said to his brothers, 'Please come near to me.' So they came near. Then he said: 'I am Joseph your brother, whom you sold into Egypt. But now, **do not therefore be grieved or angry with yourselves because you sold me here;** for God sent me before you to preserve life.' " (Gen. 45:4-5)*

Joseph's faith, persistent through severe trials, taught him peace, not anger; goodness, not evil; and love, not hate. Indeed, his faith in God had produced a harvest of fruit in his soul. Love, the fruit of the Spirit, is his reward.

> *"And now abide **faith, hope, love,** these three; but the greatest of these is love." (1 Cor. 13:13)*

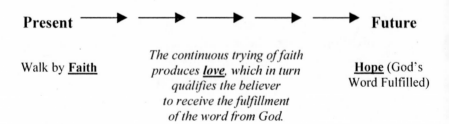

Present ➤ ➤ ➤ ➤ ➤ **Future**

Walk by **Faith**

*The continuous trying of faith produces **love**, which in turn qualifies the believer to receive the fulfillment of the word from God.*

Hope (God's Word Fulfilled)

Faith, hope and love work together. Hope is the fulfillment of God's word to us; faith is how we live now; love is the fruit of the Spirit produced in us as we walk by faith.

The Fruit of the Spirit

The word "fruit" is singular, not plural. This is lost in the English translation. However, the Greek text indicates that the fruit of the Spirit is definitely singular. There are not nine "fruits" of the Spirit, but one fruit only. The fruit of the Spirit, love, is one cluster; it is simply the many aspects and development of love. Let us use this analogy. Suppose that the fruit of the Spirit is a single ray of white light. If this white light were directed at a prism, it would be separated into seven colors of light as it passed through the glass. However, there are not seven distinct colors (rays) of light emitted. Red shades into orange; orange shades into yellow; yellow shades into green ... indigo shades into violet. There is a single spectrum comprised of many colors ranging from red to violet. So it is with the fruit of the Spirit. Love is composed of many virtues, such as joy, peace, gentleness, and longsuffering. As we undergo a transformation of our souls, the love developed by the Holy Spirit in us will be seen as joy, as peace, or as goodness. However, none of these is a separate fruit of the Spirit, for each is only a part of the whole fruit – love.

By comparing the fruit as enumerated in Galatians 5:22-23 with the famous description of love in 1 Corinthians 13:4-7, we can see that the fruit of the Spirit is one fruit but having many different flavors.

> *"But the fruit of the Spirit is **love, joy, peace, longsuffering, gentleness, goodness, faith, meekness, temperance:** against such there is no law." (Gal. 5:22-23 KJV)*

> *"**Love** suffers long and is kind; **love** does not envy; **love** does not parade itself, is not puffed up; does not behave rudely, does not seek its own, is not provoked, thinks no*

evil; does not rejoice in iniquity, but rejoices in the truth; bears all things, believes all things, hopes all things, endures all things." (1 Cor. 13:4-7)

1 Corinthians 13:4-7 is one long sentence describing the qualities of love. Love is the subject of the sentence.

Love is the sum of all the virtues, the whole (fruit).
Joy is love's strength. It rejoices not in iniquity, but rejoices in the truth. Love is glad and cheerful.
Peace is love's security. It does not envy or vaunt itself. It is quiet and confident.
Longsuffering is love's patience. It suffers long and has composure.
Gentleness is love's conduct. It bears all things, being considerate and gracious.
Goodness is love's character. It thinks no evil and hopes all things.
Faith is love's confidence. It believes all things and is constant.
Meekness is love's humility. It doesn't behave itself unseemly, is not provoked, and is comely.
Temperance is love's victory, enduring all things. This is its conquest - producing self-control.

When love gains complete mastery over our lives, its victory is self-control. This self-control binds the rest of the fruit together. When the fruit of the Spirit within is in "full bloom," the self-life is in complete submission to the Holy Spirit. The fruit of the Spirit is the complete undoing of the effects of self and sin! It results in the absence of the self-life. This is seen more clearly by now identifying the fruit of the Spirit in this manner:

Love is not thinking of self.
Joy is looking at God in spite of self.
Peace is disregarding one's loss.
Longsuffering is despising one's own hardships.
Gentleness is overlooking one's rights.
Goodness is benefiting someone else.
Faith is self-restraint.
Meekness is forgetting one's merits.
Temperance is self under control.

In an overview of the fruit of the Spirit, it should be pointed out that this list is not considered to be complete. Instead, Paul's wording for both the works of the flesh (those who practice **such things** – Gal. 5:21) and the fruit of the Spirit (Against **such** – Gal. 5:23) indicates that the list is representative, and not fully exhaustive. Paul was simply creating a list in an ad hoc manner.

Jesus' statement in John 12:24-25 is important in this discussion:

> *"Most assuredly, I say to you, unless a grain of wheat falls into the ground and dies, it remains alone; but **if it dies, it produces much grain**. He who loves his life will lose it, and he who hates his life in this world will keep it for eternal life."*

Jesus is saying that the path to fruitfulness is also the path to death of the self-life. When we let go of our own "self" life, we will gain the true "spiritual" life. This is the gospel: we should not live unto ourselves, but unto Him who died for us, and rose again (2 Cor. 5:15).

There appears to be an amazing flowing of the progressive nature of love. One virtue blends into the next. By dividing Paul's list of nine virtues (the fruit of the Spirit) into three groups of three, this becomes apparent:

Love, Joy, and Peace describe our initial experience in God, and are the first to develop in our lives.

Longsuffering, Gentleness, and Goodness are indicative of our conduct, and teach us how to relate to others.

Faith, Meekness, and Temperance control the self-life.

> *"Jesus said to him, 'You shall **love the Lord your God** with all your heart, with all your soul, and with all your mind.' This is the first and great commandment. And the second is like it: 'You shall **love your neighbor as your-self.'** On these two commandments hang all the Law and Prophets." (Matt. 22:37-40)*

Based on the above scripture and those that immediately follow, perhaps we could say that the fruit of the Spirit is loving God [thirtyfold], loving your neighbor [sixtyfold], and keeping yourself in check [hundredfold]! [Parentheses added by author.]

> *"But these are the ones sown on good ground, those who hear the word, accept it, and bear fruit: some **thirtyfold**, some **sixty**, and some a **hundred**." (Mark 4:20)*

> *"Every branch in Me that does not bear fruit He takes away; and every branch that bears **fruit** [thirtyfold] He prunes, that it may bear **more fruit** [sixtyfold])." (John 15:2) [Parentheses added by the author.]*

> *"I am the vine, you are the branches. He who abides in Me, and I in him, bears **much fruit** [hundredfold]; for*

without Me you can do nothing." (John 15:5) [Parentheses added by author]

A thirtyfold Christian is one who has an experience in God but does not know how to relate to others. A sixtyfold Christian will love God and work in relationship with others, but still remains independent and opinionated. A hundredfold Christian is one who loves God, loves his neighbor, and has died to himself.

This concept will be more fully studied in the next chapter.

Thought Questions

1. What is the difference between fruit and works?

2. How does love fulfill the requirements of the law?

3. Give a biblical definition of hope.

4. What is the relation of faith to hope?

5. A triumphant faith emerging from trial produces a character change. What is this character change?

6. Is the fruit of the Spirit singular or plural?

7. Compare the fruit of the Spirit as listed in Galatians 5: 22-23 to the description of love in 1 Corinthians 13:4-7.

8. What seems to be the three natural divisions into which Paul's list of the fruit of the Spirit falls?

Chapter Five

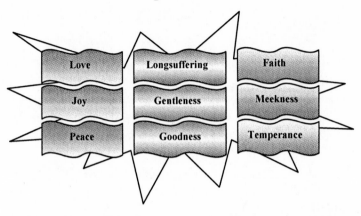

Transformed Into The Same Image

*"But we all, with unveiled face, beholding as in a mirror the glory of the Lord, are being **transformed into the same image** from glory to glory, just as by the Spirit of the Lord." (2 Cor. 3:18)*

The transformation of our lives into the image of Christ is not an instantaneous reformation. The Spirit of God accomplishes character change in us slowly but surely, taking us from glory to glory. When a measure of love for God, others, and self has been formed in us, other virtues, such as joy and peace, become evident in our lives. Our development by the Spirit is progressive; step-by-step, He works glorious changes into our lives that will remain throughout eternity.

It has been noted before that the activity of the Spirit is described as "fruit" and the activity of the flesh is referred to as "works." In the great matters of grace and law, fruit is a matter of **growth** and works require self-effort. In 2 Pet. 3:18, Peter admonishes us to *"**grow** in the grace and knowledge of our Lord and Savior Jesus Christ."*

The Christian life is not an imitation of Christ-like attitudes. It is Christ Himself, by the Holy Spirit, living His own life through yielded vessels. Christ lives in us (Gal. 2:20). The fruit of the Spirit is the expression of Christ's life being formed in us. As Jesus said, it is His peace and His joy that we possess:

> *"Peace I leave with you, **My peace** I give to you; not as the world gives do I give to you. Let not your heart be troubled, neither let it be afraid." (John 14:27)*

> *"These things I have spoken to you, that **My joy** may remain in you, and that your joy may be full." (John 15:11)*

Though the list of the fruit of the Spirit as found in Gal. 5:22-23 is not exhaustive, Paul does (perhaps, unconsciously) reveal a natural unfolding of the development of love. The fruit as listed may be divided into three groups as follows:

a)   **Love, Joy, Peace:**
our experience, first developed toward God;

b)   **Longsuffering, Gentleness, Goodness:**
our conduct toward others;

c)   **Faith, Meekness, Temperance:**
our character controlling ourselves.

The great commandment states:

> *"Jesus said to him, 'You shall love the Lord your **God** with all your heart, with all your soul, and with all your mind.' This is the first and great commandment. And the second is like it: 'You shall love your **neighbor** as **yourself**.' On these two commandments hang all the Law and the Prophets." (Matt. 22:37-40)*

The first commandment is to love God with all our heart, soul, and mind. This is reflected by love, joy, and peace. The second commandment is to love your neighbor as yourself. This is demonstrated through longsuffering, gentleness, and goodness. Faith, meekness, and temperance keep self under control. Without self under control, love for God and neighbor will be hindered.

Jesus suggested that the development of fruit is progressive. In His final talk to the disciples at the Last Supper, He spoke about **fruit**, **more fruit**, and **much fruit:**

> *"I am the true vine, and My Father is the vinedresser. Every branch in Me that does not bear fruit He takes away; and every branch that bears **fruit** He prunes, that it may bear **more fruit**. You are already clean because of the word which I have spoken to you. Abide in Me and I in you. As the branch cannot bear fruit of itself, unless it abides in the vine, neither can you, unless you abide in Me. I am the vine, you are the branches. He who abides in Me, and I in him, bears **much fruit;** for without Me you can do nothing. ... By this My Father is glorified, that you bear **much fruit;** so you will be My disciples." (John 15:1-5, 8)*

Fruit

It is interesting to note that in the discourse of the Last Supper (John 13-16), Jesus mentioned that some changes soon would take place. Among others changes, He would go away, and the Comforter would come. He, dwelling in the disciples, would lead them into all truth. That must have been a baffling new thought for them to digest. Perhaps, the disciples were somewhat bewildered by the discussion of fruit, more fruit, and much fruit. Indeed, the concept of fruit, as Jesus understood it, appeared to be foreign to their minds. The following scriptures illustrate this fact:

> *"And when His disciples James and John saw this, they said, '**Lord, do You want us to command fire to come down from heaven and consume them**, just as Elijah did?'" (Luke 9:54)*

> *"Then the mother of Zebedee's sons came to Him with her sons, kneeling down and asking something from Him. And He said to her, 'What do you wish?' She said to Him, '**Grant that these two sons of mine may sit, one on Your right hand and the other on the left, in Your kingdom.**' But Jesus answered and said, 'You do not know what you ask. Are you able to drink the cup that I am about to drink, and be baptized with the baptism that I am baptized with?' They said to Him, 'We are able.'" (Matt. 20:20-22)*

James and John appeared to lack the love that Jesus spoke about. They were ready and willing to bring destruction into the lives of others. Obviously, Zebedee's two sons, whether they had earned the positions or not, wanted to be Jesus' right hand "men" in His kingdom. Jesus, by His Spirit, would soon commence the development of fruit, then more fruit, and finally much fruit in these disciples. In the same manner, He has been transforming His disciples down through the church age.

During the Last Supper, Jesus often mentioned love, joy, and peace to the disciples – the initial experiences they would have upon entering the Spirit-filled life. Hear these words of instruction and comfort:

> *"As the Father loved Me, I also have loved you; abide in My **love**." (John 15:9)*

> *"for the Father Himself **loves** you, because you have loved Me, and have believed that I came forth from God." (John 16:27)*

> *"But now I come to you, and these things I speak in the world, that they may have My **joy** fulfilled in themselves." (John 17:13)*

> *"Until now you have asked nothing in My name. Ask, and you will receive, that your **joy** may be full." (John 16:24)*

> *"Therefore you now have sorrow; but I will see you again and your heart will rejoice, and your **joy** no one will take from you." (John 16:22)*

> *"Most assuredly, I say to you that you will weep and lament, but the world will rejoice; and you will be sorrowful, but your sorrow will be turned into **joy**." (John 16:20)*

> *"These things I have spoken to you, that My joy may remain in you, and that your **joy** may be full." (John 15:11)*

> *"These things I have spoken to you, that in Me you may have **peace**. In the world you will have tribulation; but be of good cheer, I have overcome the world." (John 16:33)*

> *"**Peace** I leave with you, My peace I give to you; not as the world gives do I give to you. Let not your heart be troubled, neither let it be afraid." (John 14:27)*

Numerous are the texts in the Last Supper that speak of the love relationship between the Father and Son, and toward the disciples. Notice the emphasis on love, joy, and peace, the first triad of the fruit of the Spirit. Jesus knew that these virtues would be their initial experiences in the Holy Spirit. Also, note that Jesus had nothing to say concerning the second and third triads of fruit – from longsuffering to self-control. He knew that the disciples could not grasp further discussion at this point. The Holy Spirit would develop them beyond His initial instructions and comments.

Many Christians never develop beyond the first triad. They do not permit the Holy Spirit to work longsuffering, gentleness, and goodness into their character. Consequently, they do not know how to work out relationships with other people. They remain thirtyfold Christians and bear very little fruit for God.

To show that this love was to flow through them to others, Jesus said:

*"A new commandment I give to you, that you love one another; as I have loved you, that you also love one another. By this all will know that you are My disciples, **if you have love one for another**." (John 13:34-35)*

More fruit

*"If someone says, 'I love God,' and hates his brother, he is a liar; for he who does not love his brother whom he has seen, how can he love God whom he has not seen? And this commandment we have from Him: **that he who loves God must love his brother also**." (I John 4:20-21)*

God is not satisfied when we only experience His love for us. We love God because He first loved us. However, since God receives greater glory when our love for Him is expressed toward others, He commands us to love others. John actually declared that if we do not love others, we are not submissive to the work of the Spirit in our hearts.

In John 15:2, Jesus said, *" ... every branch that bears fruit He prunes, that it may bear more fruit."* God the Father, the vinedresser, is the One who applies the pruning shears to our lives, cutting away those undesirable character traits that hinder the development of longsuffering (and consequently, gentleness and goodness). Thus, our stifled relationships with others are freed to develop, delighting the Lord and benefiting others and ourselves.

How does the Lord accomplish this progress in character development? He allows our private relationships with Him to be invaded by other people. Since the next group of fruit commences with longsuffering, He lets us experience some of it. People infringe on our time, bring accusations against us, irritate us with their nonsense, and make our lives generally uncomfortable. Indeed, the fruit known as longsuffering is well named: there appears to be no end to the annoyance. The quick remedies we seek are dismal failures; and the sources of irritation renew their vitality. The sandpaper the Lord provides is of excellent quality - the kind that never seems to wear out!

"God, this is not enjoyable anymore," you complain.
"Hold on my beloved!" He exclaims, "This is the most expedient way to get you from **fruit** to **more fruit**."
 "But, I'm not sure I want to get to ...."
"Hold on! Hold on! The love I am imparting to you will bless many!"

God knows all about sandpaper; we are His sandpaper. We give Him ample reason to be annoyed with us, but He still brings us benefit and kindness. In the midst of our selfishness and disobedience, He anoints with gifts and provides His glorious presence. There is no better example of longsuffering.

While we often consider longsuffering and patience to be synonymous, there is a slight difference in meaning. Biblically speaking, patience deals with circumstances and longsuffering has to do with people. When dealing with a financial problem (circumstance) we must be patient. However, an irritating younger brother requires longsuffering.

Patience, a cousin of longsuffering, is seen throughout scripture as a virtue that has power to bring change into an individual's life. Patience brings forth perfection, wholeness, so that we lack nothing, becoming complete. It gives experience and proven character (James 1:2-4; Rom. 5:3-5).

Thus, in order to bear **more fruit**, to develop more fully, to become free of our unconscious self-centeredness, we are pruned and our love is tested. We are called to be longsuffering. We learn to forbear, and gentleness and goodness will grow in our lives as we submit to Christ.

Much Fruit

We have not yet come to perfection. The Father is glorified if we bear **much fruit** (John 15:8). There remains the third triad of faith, meekness, and temperance. Further pruning is brought into our lives. This time, the Father applies His pruning shears deftly and snips away at all that is left of our self-centeredness. We can love God and others for selfish motives. Thus, this triad grows by first trying our faith. (There is some discussion as to whether this fruit should be called faithfulness in the sense of loyalty, but the Greek word indicates that faith is the correct translation. The King James Version of the Bible uses "faith.")

As believers, we must be convinced that God is in control. However, as we are being pruned, many times our world gets turned upside down, and we wonder if God really is in control. Our environment and outer circumstances change. Situations seem to get out of control, and we are powerless to do anything about them.

Do we give up in despair? In the midst of it all, is there a conviction rising within that God is our shield? Do we know God is sovereign? Is He in control? Do we stand strong? Will we go with what we feel and think, or trust what God has said?

The conviction that God is in control will enable us to realize that God is working something in us. He is changing us so that the self-life will be mastered. Meekness is the ability to be taught by another. Temperance is the result. This conviction that controls the Christian's life allows us to be meek and gives us strength for temperance. John confirms that this is death to self – the much fruit spoken of by Jesus:

> *"Most assuredly, I say to you, unless a grain of wheat falls into the ground and dies, it remains alone; but if it dies, it produces* **much** *grain. He who loves his life will lose it, and he who hates his life in this world will keep it for eternal life." (John 12:24-25)*

It seems, according to Mark's version of the parable of the sower (Mark 4:14-20), that there will be some believers who will never progress beyond the initial experience with God. They simply will not learn relationships with others, and remain thirtyfold Christians. Some will develop healthy relationships with others, and become sixtyfold believers. But, thankfully, there are others who will be hundredfold disciples of Christ, who will love God, love their neighbors, and die to self.

> *"But these are the ones sown on good ground, those who hear the word, accept it, and bear fruit:* **some thirtyfold, some sixty, and some a hundred.** *" (Mark 4:20)*

According to Luke's version of the same parable (Luke 8:4-15), the end result is achieved by patience, and patience brings forth fruit to "maturity."

> *"But the ones that fell on the good ground are those who, having heard the word with a noble and good heart, keep it and bear fruit with* **patience.** *" (Luke 8:15)*

An overview of the truths taught in this chapter may be seen in the following chart:

Fruit	More Fruit	Much Fruit
Towards God	**Towards Others**	**Control of Self**
30 – fold	**60 – fold**	**100 - fold**
Love	Longsuffering	Faith
Joy	Gentleness	Meekness
Peace	Goodness	Temperance

Thought Questions

1. Can you identify various stages of growth in your own life?

2. How fully did Jesus expound on the fruit of the Spirit during the Last Supper?

3. Why is pruning necessary?

4. How has God brought pruning into your life? How have you responded to it?

5. Do you have a desire to bear much fruit? To be a hundredfold Christian?

Chapter Six

Seed And Soil

Many familiar scriptures liken the believer to a fruit-bearing tree, a garden, the planting of the Lord, or a spring of water that never fails. Isaiah used beautiful imagery in penning these descriptions of God's people:

> *"To console those who mourn in Zion, To give them beauty for ashes, The oil of joy for mourning, The garment of praise for the spirit of heaviness; That they may be called **the trees of righteousness, The planting of the Lord**, that He may be glorified." (Isa. 61:3)*

> *"The Lord will guide you continually, And satisfy your soul in drought, And strengthen your bones; You shall be like a **watered garden**, And like a **spring of water**, whose waters do not fail." (Isa. 58:11)*

The apostle Paul employed the same literary skill to picture the church, using words like planted, watered, and increase:

*"I **planted**, Apollos **watered**, but God gave **the increase**. So then neither he who plants is anything, nor he who waters, but God who gives the increase. Now he who plants and he who waters are one, and each will receive his own reward according to his own labor. For we are God's fellow workers; you are God's **field**, you are God's building." (1 Cor. 3:6-9)*

Undoubtedly, it is God's will for us to bear fruit – not just fruit, or more fruit, but **much** fruit (John 15:2,5,8,16). Paul prayed for the Colossians as follows:

*"For this reason we also, since the day we heard it, do not cease to pray for you, and to ask that you may be filled with the knowledge of His will in all wisdom and spiritual understanding; that you may walk worthy of the Lord, fully pleasing to Him, being **fruitful** in every good work and **increasing** in the knowledge of God;" (Col. 1:9-10)*

Besides preaching the very familiar parable of the sower, Jesus also taught the parable of the seed:

*"And He said, 'The Kingdom of God is as if a man should scatter seed on the ground, and should sleep by night and rise by day, and the seed should sprout and grow, he himself does not know how. For the earth yields crops by itself: first the **blade**, then the **head**, after that **the full grain** in the head. But when the grain ripens, immediately he puts in the sickle, because the harvest has come.' " (Mark 4:26-29)*

Earlier in this chapter, Jesus identified the seed as the "*word*" (Mark 4:14). The word of God is the key to the development of the fruit of the Spirit in our lives. This short parable teaches that the word of God is living and powerful (c.f. Heb. 4:12). The word of God, as spoken by the Holy Spirit, is living and has power to produce fruit; but how it does this is a mystery to us. In the Colossian experience, it was the word of the truth of the gospel that brought forth fruit in them, evidenced by their love in the Spirit (Col. 1:5-8). Likewise, the Thessalonians learned that when the word of God is received, not as the word of men, but as the word of God, it effectually works in those who believe (1 Thess. 2:13).

James admonishes us that we are to receive the *"engrafted word"* that is able to save our souls (James 1:21-22). The word "engrafted" means that which has been implanted will germinate and grow, will sprout and produce, will spring up. The same Greek word was translated *"sprang up"* in Luke's version of the parable of the sower (Luke 8:6). When the word of God is received into our hearts (heard and obeyed), it will progressively change our character.

As we submit to the word, we are changed. The word produces fruit: first the blade, then the head, and then the full grain in the head. This triad of growth stages can certainly be likened to the thirtyfold, sixtyfold, and hundredfold fruit in the parable of the sower (Mk 4:20). Overall, it can be seen as a foreshadowing of the nature of the fruit of the Spirit: loving God, loving others, and finally, conquering self.

We are born again by the incorruptible seed of the word of God (1 Pet. 1:23). This is also how faith is imparted; Rom: 10:17 states, *"So then faith comes by hearing, and hearing by the word of God."* Jesus, knowing the power of His word, placed great emphasis on it as He spoke to His disciples at the Last Supper (John 15:1-8). He told them that as they abide in Him and He in them, they would produce much fruit. Actually, the progression from fruit to much fruit happens as a result of abiding in Him. The word also cleanses and purges those who abide in Christ.

How does Christ abide in His disciples? How can this be a practical reality?

> *"In the beginning was the **Word**, and the Word was with God, and the Word was God. He [Jesus] was in the beginning with God." (John 1:1-2) [Parenthesis added by author]*

Since **Jesus is the Word**, He abides in his disciples if His word abides in them. Therefore, allowing the word of God to abide in our hearts permits Christ to abide there:

> *"... He who abides in Me, and **I in him**, bears much fruit: ..." (John 15:5)*

> *"If you abide in Me, and **My words abide in you**, you will ask what you desire, and it shall be done for you." (John 15:7)*

Notice what Jesus said in these two verses. The phrases in bold type have similar positions in the two verses. In effect, Jesus has stated that **I** and **My words** signify the same person.

The word "abide" means to stay, be present, dwell, remain, and continue. The words of Christ must be comfortable in our hearts. His words are welcome, and because we submit to them, we are "at ease" with the word of God.

Now, having considered the nature of the word of God as a seed, let us turn our attention to the matter of the soil, the condition of our hearts into which the seed is sown. The parable of the sower as related by Mark is provided below:

> *"Listen! Behold, a sower went out to sow. And it happened, as he sowed, that some seed fell by the wayside; and the birds of the air came and devoured it. Some fell on stony ground, where it did not have much earth; and immediately it sprang up because it had no depth of earth. But when the sun was up it was scorched, and because it had no root it withered away. And some seed fell among the thorns; and the thorns grew up and choked it, and it yielded no crop. But other seed fell on good ground and yielded a crop that sprang up, increased and produced: some thirtyfold, some sixty, and some a hundred." (Mark 4:3-8)*

The parable of the sower is preserved by the three synoptic gospels (Matt. 13:3-9, 18-23; Mark 4:3-8, 14-20; Luke 8:5-8, 11-15). Each gospel writer relates the parable in a slightly different way, making it serve the particular need of his intended readers. For our purposes, we will create a composite from the three gospels.

The Wayside

Parable: After the seed was sown, fowls of the air came and devoured them, for the ground was trodden down.

Interpretation: The word is not understood, and the wicked one, Satan, the devil, comes immediately and takes or catches away the word that was sown in the hearts of the people, lest they should believe and be saved.

Matthew emphasizes the need to understand the word of God. It must be comprehended and considered. Time must be given to meditate upon it, and to have it search out and influence the heart. The enemy of souls is referred to as the wicked one, who must rob the word from the heart in hot haste. Mark says that Satan must do this immediately, because he knows that there is power in the living word of God. Satan must get rid of its influence as quickly as possible. Luke emphasizes the hardness of men's hearts. The way is trodden down. A continuous walk of sin has caused the heart to become calloused. Carelessness and indifference have taken their toll. Often, in these cases, a crisis is needed to plough up such a hardened heart. The devil's goal is to disallow the word of God any influence in the heart of man, preventing his salvation. In similar language, Paul later wrote that the god of this age blinds the minds of those that believe not, lest the light of the gospel would shine unto them (2 Cor. 4:4). Obviously, the experience of salvation is the first step in bearing the much fruit that glorifies God.

The Stony Place

Parable: In the stony place, there is not much earth, and the seed springs up immediately. Because there is not much depth, it lacks moisture. The sun scorches the plant that is without root, and it withers away.

Interpretation: There are some who receive the word with joy and gladness, but have no root in themselves. They believe and endure for a while, but in the time of tribulation, affliction, temptation, and persecution arising because of the word, they are sooner or later offended and fall away.

When the heart is still a stony place, there may appear to be quick and apparent growth. Although it is not pleasant, a time of trial is necessary for real growth. The plant needs heat. However, where there are no roots, heat kills the plant; it shrivels and dries up. We are to be rooted and built up in Christ Jesus (Col. 2:6-7). Christ is to dwell in our hearts by faith, so that we might be rooted and grounded in love (Eph. 3:17). Thus, the time of heat and trial will strengthen us instead of shaking us. Without roots, no nourishment can be received. Growth is impossible.

Without commitment to the word of God, no development will take place. Many who initially receive the blessings of the gospel embrace sensationalism, and actually remain self-centered. The experience never reaches the inner motivations, and the mind, will, emotions, and conscience remain unaltered. Nevertheless, they endure for a time, and enjoy a season of privileges and gracious influences.

However, the trial of faith is necessary for growth and development. Pressure causes one to grow. As Jesus said, purging and pruning is the way to greater fruitfulness (John 15:2). Trials will come, for the world hates the gospel because it exposes its sins and shortcomings. When the pressure is on, those with stony hearts are immediately offended. They become tripped up, and stumble. They refrain from walking with the Lord, withdraw themselves and desert the gospel, not having allowed the word to go deeper into their lives.

The Thorny Place

Parable: In this ground, thorns grow and choke the seed, so that no fruit comes forth.

Interpretation: Though some believers will go forth, the
cares of this world, the deceitfulness of riches, and the pleasures
of this life, choke the word so that it brings forth no fruit to perfection. Thorns stifle the word of God. They strangle it completely. There is competition for nourishment. Will the spiritual
life suffer because of the pursuit of worldly pleasures? There are
two extremes. One is anxiety about our needs, and the other is a
desire for riches. The heart needs to learn to be content with
God's supply for our needs. Christ Himself is our satisfying portion. Riches never satisfy. They deceive and delude us with their
lies. The soul of man was not created to be satisfied with things.
Jesus made it very plain that man cannot serve both God and
mammon (Matt. 6:24-34). Paul also warned about the destructive power this has on one's soul (1 Tim. 6:9-10).

A person receives the gospel, and starts to pursue growth as a
Christian. Attachment to the temporary things of this present life
with its lusts and desires competes for the limited time and energy of man. The lust of the flesh, the lust of the eyes, and the
pride of life choke the wonderful working of the word of God so
that it is not given place (1 John 2: 15-17). In this life, the will of
God remains for the most part undone, even though that will has
been made plain to the believer. The Christian life is more of a
hobby than the center of existence. Fruit is not brought to completion. It never blossoms into fullness, and is never finished,
illustrative of a carnal man.

The Good Ground

Parable: In the good ground, there are those who will
spring up and bear fruit: some thirtyfold, some sixtyfold, and
some hundredfold.

Interpretation: There are those that understand the word of God, and they receive and keep it with an honest and good heart. With patience, fruit increases.

Matthew once again emphasizes the need to understand the word. However, his order of thirtyfold, sixtyfold, and hundredfold indicates that even in good ground there are those who will not reach their potential in God, and fall short of fullness. Mark speaks of the necessity to receive the word, to accept it, to delight in it, and to admit its influence. He thus speaks of the fruit in a progressive manner, increasing from thirtyfold to sixtyfold to hundredfold. As one submits to the word of God, there is growth and enlargement. Luke emphasizes an honest and good heart, speaking of both the outward appearance and inward character. He encourages his readers to keep the word, and to hold it fast. This will produce perfection in an enduring and constant manner.

Each gospel writer makes a particular emphasis. Matthew's strongest contrast is between the good ground and the wayside. Thus he emphasizes the need to **understand** the word of God. However, understanding by itself is not enough to ensure perfection. Of those who understand, some develop thirtyfold, some sixtyfold, and some hundredfold. Mark seems to contrast the good ground against the stony places. He thus emphasizes the need to **receive** the word of God. Those who receive in addition to understanding have more potential to develop. Mark's order is identical to Matthew's, but not all will progress to yield fullness. Luke contrasts most strongly the good ground against the thorny soil, thus emphasizing the need to **keep** the word. He makes no mention of progress, but only speaks of the hundredfold, of perfection. Those whose hearts are honest and good,

who have removed the thorns from the field of the heart, will
with patience come to the full harvest of fruit.

In comparing the three gospels, note the progression from **understanding** the word, to **receiving** the word, to **keeping** it.
This is the path to fruitfulness, that the word of God would have
free and complete sway over the heart. Saints, it is our duty to
give place to the word of God, to receive it with meekness, to
submit to its principles, and to obey it in every area of our lives.
May we be fruitful in every good work!

Thought Questions

1. What are some examples of imagery the scripture uses to illustrate the concept of fruit bearing?

2. What is the relation between the word of God and fruit bearing?

3. How does God's word abide in our hearts?

4. How can we prepare the soil of our hearts?

5. According to the parable of the sower, what conditions must exist for the greatest fruitfulness? What are our responsibilities to ensure this fruitfulness?

.

Chapter Seven

Love

The fruit of the Spirit is **love**. Joy, peace, longsuffering, gentleness, goodness, faith, meekness, and temperance describe the development of love as it grows, deepens, and matures. Love is the foundation of the Christian life, and by it, the church will be edified and brought into maturity. By love we are to serve one another, for all the laws of God are summed up in it (Gal. 5:5-6, 13-14).

> *" from whom the whole body, joined and knit together by what every joint supplies, according to the effective working by which every part does its share, causes growth of the body for the edifying of itself in **love**."*
> *(Eph. 4:16)*

The Greek language, from which the New Testament is translated, has several words for the one English word "love." To understand the fruit of love, it will be very beneficial to define these Greek words, so that the biblical teaching will not be confused. The first two words are not found in the New Testament,

but were part of the Greek language of the time. These words
are:

Eros – This is sensual love, predominately physical and based
on passion. It can refer to an animal magnetism and includes
sexual expressions. Eros is a good servant in the marriage covenant, but it is a bad master. Passions can turn quickly. Sexual
love needs to be controlled by the will for useful purposes. An
excellent example of eros love controlling a relationship is that
of Amnon, who lusted after his half-sister, Tamar. Once he had
forced her, his passion turned to hatred (2 Sam. 13).

Storge – This is domestic love, and refers to family ties and relationships. It is seen in the love of a mother for her baby, or the
care of a sister for another sister. It is the bonding and kinship of
family.

Phileo – This is human friendship, and refers to a warm, inti-
mate relationship of mind and heart. It is a union of ideals and
values. However, ideals and values may change. Therefore this
love can fade with changing circumstances. Phileo love usually
embraces a narrow circle, showing fondness and natural affection one to another. Sometimes, this love is substituted in
churches for the fruit of the Spirit, and fellowship is then fos-
tered along social needs and desires. The anointing which breaks
down all barriers and social distinctions, uniting the Body of
Christ, is relegated to oblivion. Misunderstandings in the church
flourish when phileo love replaces agape love.

Agape – This is the fruit of the Spirit - divine love. It is a biblical word, not found in Greek literature other than the New Testament. It describes God's character and nature, for God is love
(1 John 4:8). Agape love has been defined as an eternal will to
all goodness. As one is born again and filled with the Spirit, the

nature of Christ Himself is imparted in the heart, causing one to know and experience God's love. To describe this love, Christians resurrected an obsolete word (agape) and gave it a new definition. It is used to describe the essence of what God Himself is. It is love that loves because of its own inherent nature, not because of the excellence or worthiness of its object. It is like a seed in the sense that within that seed is the power to produce fruit. Love's nature is to grow, develop, and become the blessing and joy of everything that wants it. It is love that has no dependence on emotion, but is controlled by the will. When agape love pervades the other types of love (eros, storge, phileo), it brings all of one's relationships into full bloom and meaning.

For a moment, let's consider the Father's plan for His Son. Once this is seen, the beauty and importance of the fruit of the Spirit will become even more pronounced. The human race was created in the image and likeness of God to produce an eternal companion for His Son. Christ came for the purpose of giving birth to the church, which is His Body, and thus obtaining His Bride. In light of God's eternal purpose, the development and training of the church is the present task of the Holy Spirit. The Body of Christ is being prepared for its eternal destiny of ruling and reigning with Christ.

Prayer is better understood from this perspective. Prayer is the arena where the techniques, skills, know-how, etc. are learned and developed for rulership with Christ. This is God's ultimate goal for the praying church. Suffering is also better understood from this perspective. Though suffering is a consequence of the fall, it will produce the character, disposition, and the compassionate spirit that will be required for rulership with Christ. It decentralizes self, and causes one to learn the love of God, putting one into the same mind and heart as Christ in His kingdom.

In God's eternal purpose, love is the essential qualification for the exercise of authority in the kingdom of heaven. In the manifestation of that kingdom at the Lord's appearing, love will rule. The kingdom, administered by the Holy Spirit, is already here in principle; and training in agape love is the great business of this present life. God allows tribulations now so that we might be decentralized from self, and more fruitful in the deep dimensions of agape love. Those dimensions of agape love are the fruit of the Spirit that originates in, flows from, and is characterized by God Himself.

The great revelation of the church as unfolded on the pages of the New Testament shows that the church is edified and built up when the church learns agape love. All other means of edification, such as the gifts of the Spirit, relate only to this temporal world, and will not be taken into eternity (1 Cor. 13). Love is eternal in nature, and not temporal. Therefore, the great need is love. It is the goal of the Christian life, and prepares the church for its eternal destiny as the Bride of Christ, ruling and reigning with Him.

God has designed that the church be edified by the members expressing agape love one toward the other (1 Cor. 8:1). It is the key to unity (Eph. 4:2-3), and it will heal any problem that exists in the church (1 Pet. 4:8). With this in mind, a quick survey of various epistles will show love indeed is the goal the church is to pursue, preparing it for its glorious destiny.

Romans – While both Jews and Gentiles had been saved, their different backgrounds did not allow them to accept each other. Therefore, exhortations to love one another without hypocrisy, and to be affectionately joined together in brotherly love are expressed. Love will not work ill toward its neighbor. In this way, a church comprised of people with different backgrounds, cultures, temperaments, religious persuasions, opinions, and various stages of growth, would not fall apart. Instead, there would be kindness, patience, and seeking of like-mindedness among the saints for the benefit of all.

The development of the Body of Christ is the climax to the Roman epistle. The discussion of the salvation of God (1–8) leads to the revelation of the purpose of God, that Christ would be the firstborn among many brethren (8:28-30). This purpose of God is then expounded in terms of the Body of Christ in chapter 12. The remainder of the epistle (13-16) shows how the fruit of the Spirit bonds the church together in love, overcoming all differences by the triumphant work of the Holy Spirit.

Galatians – What happens to righteousness if the law is removed? Paul's answer is that the Spirit will insure righteousness. The Holy Spirit produces an ethical life change that the law demands but cannot create. Love is the fulfillment of the law, and a loving church fulfills the heart of God. A church truly submitted to the Holy Spirit walks in love.

Philippians – This church was known for its warmth and open heart, but was failing to let love be guided by knowledge and judgment. Minor problems, such as murmuring, were beginning to develop. If left unattended, they would explode into major divisions later. Love requires the renewing of the mind as well as that of the heart if division is to be avoided.

James – James wrote his epistle to his Jewish brethren, and lifted love as the "royal law." He pointed out that this law brings liberty, and is demonstrated by good works of faith.

Colossians – The Colossians were praised for their love in the Spirit, which would bring them into "perfection:" full maturity, completeness, and standing complete in the will of God. Love being present, God could guide the church in many areas not otherwise possible.

Ephesians - Being rooted and grounded in love, these believers would experience the knowledge of God. The fruit of the Spirit is the key to unity and the way to develop corporately as the Body of Christ.

1 Corinthians – Several problems were apparent in the Corinthian church. Divisiveness, pride, self-exaltation, fornication, position seeking, and taking each other to court only starts the list!

Paul's famous description of love in Chapter 13 demonstrates that none of these many problems would exist if the church walked in love. This description of love, and how it applies to the Corinthian problem, is worked out in detail in the next chapter of this book.

Thought Questions

1. Define the four Greek words for love.

2. In your opinion, are some churches guilty of building fellowship around phileo love instead of agape love?

3. What is the eternal destiny of the church? For what is it being prepared? How do prayer and suffering relate to this destiny?

4. Love is the essential qualification for the exercise of authority in the kingdom of heaven. What does this mean?

5. Participating in relationships as members of the one Body of Christ provides the arena where agape love is learned and practiced. Prayerfully read through the epistles mentioned in this chapter from this perspective. Are you able to see nuggets of truth that were hidden before?

Chapter Eight

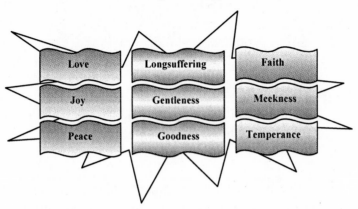

Love Is Needed At Corinth

According to Acts 18, Paul spent eighteen months at Corinth. Though there was much persecution, God gave the apostle many converts. Secular, non-biblical sources suggest that as many as 60,000 people were won to the Lord. That is one-tenth of the population of the city at that time.

In the Acts narrative, one of the converts named Crispus was a ruler in a synagogue. He befriended Paul, and permitted him to preach in the synagogue. The unbelieving Jews collectively showed opposition and forced Paul out from their midst. Then Paul preached from a place provided by Justus, another of his friends. His labors from there brought about the conversion of many Gentiles (Acts 18:8). This mighty revival produced many offshoots and led to the founding of churches, not only in Corinth, but also in the regions of Cenchrea and Achaia (c.f. 2 Cor. 1:1; Rom. 16:1).

The makeup of the Corinthian church was diverse. Many converts had no religious training and some were deep into idolatry prior to conversion. Paul loved the Corinthians with intense affection, but they were the most problematic of all the churches. They were proud, egotistical, opinionated, divisive, suspicious, immoral, indifferent to Paul's sufferings, contemptuous regarding his teachings, and tolerant of his enemies. Dishonesty, drunkenness, and sensuality were present within the church. Obviously, many of the Corinthians came from very immoral backgrounds, including heathen worship that majored on sexual activities.

Paul wrote this letter to the Corinthians while in the midst of a great "revival" occurring in Asia, primarily centered in Ephesus (Acts 19). He had received an evil report of the church from Apollos, who had ministered there after Paul left. He received additional information from Corinthian church members who visited him while he was at Ephesus (the household of Chloe – 1 Cor. 1:11). The Corinthians had sent Paul a letter containing several questions, some of which were generated by genuine perplexity, but others by unhealthy speculations. Paul's letter was written in response to their less-than-honorable behavior and to answer their questions.

It is in this context that the great "love chapter" should be read. Otherwise, much of 1 Cor. 13 will appear more devotional than practical. Love is the more excellent way. The church had experienced much of the grace of God. In God's providence, a variety of ministries had been sent to them. They had overwhelmingly experienced the grace of God, being called by Him, all of which was confirmed by the presence of the spiritual gifts in their midst (1 Cor. 1:4-9).

A quick reading of the entire book will reveal that this particular church had more than its share of inner turmoil. In this light, the "love chapter" becomes a very central focus. Paul's answer to the church's difficulties is found in his description of love as unfolded throughout Chapter 13. Though not an exhaustive list of all its difficulties, the following problems may be ascertained from a quick skimming of the book:

o Divisiveness over different teachers (1:10-13)
o Immaturity and carnality (3:1-3, 13:11)
o Deception (3:18)
o Judgmental attitude (4:3-5; 9:1-3)
o Pride and position-seeking (4:6)
o Gross immorality (5:1-2)
o Disputes leading to secular court (6:1-8)
o Impurity in believers (6:9-10)
o Fornication (6:13-20)
o Questions about marriage – indicative of potential problems and desires (7)
o Offending weaker brethren (8; 10:23-33)
o Idolatry, fornication, murmurings (10:7-10, 14)
o Contentions due to Judaistic teachers concerning the role of women (11:2-16; 14:34-35)
o Abuse of love-feasts and the Lord's Supper (11:17-34)
o Not discerning the Lord's Body (11:29)
o Failure to judge self (11:31)
o Abuse of Gifts of the Spirit, centering on pride, self-exaltation, self-gratification, and divisiveness (12 & 14)
o Less visible gifts and ministries looked down upon (12:15-27)
o Desire to be preeminent (12:28-30)
o Lack of order and purpose in the church meetings, resulting in no mutual edification (14:26)
o Not teachable, desiring rather to remain in ignorance (14:38)

o   Doubts concerning their hope (resurrection) which
    led to loose living (15:31-34)
o   Without being fixed upon their hope, the work of
    God no longer held priority and importance (15:58)

The above list reveals the emptiness of this "spiritual" church.
The Corinthians held a mistaken notion concerning the meaning
of spirituality. By their definition, spirituality meant only outward displays of power, which, by the grace of God, they had
experienced. However, their emphasis was misplaced, as so often is the case in modern day believers. All too often, the gospel
is presented in a way that makes it appealing to fallen man.
There is more concern with satisfying the needs of man than
there is for the glory of God.

According to Paul, a walk of love (fruit of the Spirit) demonstrates life in the Spirit. The Christian life is never a question of
whether one is to follow the gifts or the fruit. The church is to
follow the Spirit, who both empowers and gives character. As
any individual seeks to love, the love of God will manifest itself
in the gifts, resulting in a more powerful and positive effect. For
instance, love will express itself in speaking edification, exhortation, and comfort, thus, prophesying. Compassion will pray for
the sick, thus releasing gifts of healings. The gifts of the Spirit
will flow quite naturally out of a heart that expresses itself in
love. Love for God and others, the two commandments upon
which hang all the law and the prophets, is to be the primary focus. Love for others, including the lost, will seek the power of
God on their behalf, and thus gifts of the Spirit express and ex-
tend that love.

However, the practical application of these concepts is of the
utmost importance. While inspirational, Paul intended this description of love to be practical to his readers. As will be dem-

onstrated, the many problems that existed in Corinth could have been avoided if the correct definition of love had been understood and pursued. With this in mind, read the "love chapter" in light of the Corinthian need and misplaced emphasis.

Love is defined in 1 Corinthians 13:4-8 as follows:

Suffers long – This means to passively endure, to be long-spirited, able to forbear, to have long patience with other people. Throughout the epistle, Paul exhibits this characteristic of love. Note that longsuffering is the first of Paul's descriptions, for the Corinthians needed to receive each other, though they may have come from various backgrounds and displayed different temperaments.

Kind – Kindness has progressed beyond longsuffering. It means to actively do good things to those with whom one has been longsuffering. It is to be benevolent, to show oneself useful, gracious, and pleasant. In other words, one does not become irritable when one's longsuffering is tested! The Corinthians missed this definition of spirituality. They were intent on pulling down each other and closed to those of different persuasions.

Does not envy – Love does not hold grudges, nor is it jealous. Love is neither indignant nor pained at seeing excellence in another. The lack of this characteristic led the Corinthian church into schisms. This misconception of spirituality actually caused them to pursue a less-than-spiritual path. Although definitely unprepared for the task, everybody wanted to be an apostle!

Does not parade itself – Love does not show off or brag. It never displays self-importance. It neither boasts nor knows vainglory. A person who loves will never say to a lesser that he is not needed. Much of the Corinthian problem stemmed from the lack of this characteristic of love (12:20-24; 3:16-18; 10:12; and 14:37). The Corinthians needed to know that all members were important regardless of function and status. They were wise in their own eyes, self-deceived, and assumed spirituality though their characteristics betrayed them.

Is not puffed up – Love is not proud or arrogant. It is not conceited nor inflated with ego. It is not blown up with haughtiness. Were the Corinthians puffed up? Were they full of "empty talk" or was there substance to their appearance? This fault led to their own false sense of self-importance over the ministries God permitted them to receive, as demonstrated in 4:6-7, 18-19. It directly led to fornication (5:2) and egotism (8:1-2). Their "spirituality" was very carnal! With this attitude, they improperly used the gifts, bringing division into the church by the gifts that should have brought unity.

Doesn't behave rudely– Love is unselfish and sympathetic. It is courteous, and shows itself in proper behavior to the appropriate people. The Corinthians failed in these characteristics as shown in 7:36, regarding marriage. This lack of love was responsible for the behavior described in 12:23 and 14:40. The prophets would speak out of turn, without any sense of respect for the others. The lack of this characteristic showed itself as the love-feasts were abused by the wealthier who didn't share with those less fortunate, and turned a holy time of fellowship into a drunken party. Since some were about to deny the resurrection, it led to loose behavior and the philosophy of the world which states, *"Let us eat and drink, for tomorrow we die."* (15:31-34)

Does not seek its own – Love is selfless in attitude and conduct, and seeks the happiness of others. Wouldn't a church full of love consider the weaker members rather than offend them? Wouldn't such a group of believers see to it that each judged himself, not becoming a stumbling block for others? Wouldn't the Body of the Lord be discerned? Surely then the gifts of the Spirit would function in an edifying manner. Read 8:9-12, 10:24-33, and 11:29,31 in the light of this characteristic of love to see some new light on spirituality.

Is not provoked – Love simply is not stirred to anger. However, the Corinthians failed again. There were contentions over teachers and leaders (1:11), length of hair, and about women (11:16).

Thinks no evil – This means much more than not to have a bad thought about someone. More accurately, it means that love doesn't keep a record of wrongs done against it. It never takes an inventory of hurts. A person walking in love will not live, act, or react out of offences and wounds. A believer walking in love does not cease to act in kindness because an offence was received from a person. Love even blesses enemies. What about the Corinthians who took each other to court? Love, which thinks no evil, does not keep records of wounds and offences so as to retaliate or fail to bless.

Does not rejoice in iniquity – Here, iniquity means "unrighteousness," that which is not right, either in relation to God or man. Love is not happy where sin is, and is not glad at the misfortune of others. There is no joy when another fails or falls. How, then, can a church have fornication and divisions unchecked (1:12; 3:3-4; 5:1-5; 6:9-10)?

Rejoices in the truth – A believer walking in the love that the Spirit births, seeks honesty. This love looks for purity and cleanliness of lives and relationships. It wants things to be genuine, without hypocrisy.

Bears all things – Love endures wrongs and evils done against it and then covers them. It hides the infirmities of others, and covers them up in silence. The Greek word is akin to "roof" and it suggests preservation by covering. It never speaks from a wounded heart that is determined to expose the injustice done against it. The heart's attitude is always to restore.

Believes all things – Love will take the best, kindest, and most positive view possible. It searches for the good, and gives the benefit of the doubt. It has faith in all people.

Hopes all things – Someone who walks in love believes the best of all people and circumstances, takes a bright and cheery view, and finds reason for confidence.

Endures all things – Love never fails in its work. It preserves, undergoes anything, and bears up courageously.

Love never fails – Love will never be pulled off the stage as a bad act. Every single problem at Corinth boiled down to failure in love. All difficulties could have been resolved if the church had corrected its definition of spirituality.

As easily observed by the Corinthian example, a wrong concept of spirituality leads to a host of abuses in attitudes and actions. Spirituality is never a choice between power and character. Pursuing love, as commanded in 14:1, does not mean to hold the gifts in reserve. That simply is not the case, but the gifts should not be given priority, as if spirituality is summed up in them. When love is evident, the gifts will function spontaneously from a heart of compassion, and thus will have edified. Follow love, and all the provisions God has given for life in the present will be in proper perspective. Knowledge apart from love works against spirituality (8:1). The same goes for every expression of the Spirit apart from love. It is the more excellent way (12:31). All that is done is to be in the context of love (16:14).

This same love is to be reproduced in the church. Spirituality in the sight of God is determined by love for Him and each other. Love will not fail in its work to see the church through turmoil, to bring it into maturity, the fullness of Christ. In this manner, the church not only will flourish powerfully in the gifts of the Spirit, but also will bring lasting edification.

Thought Questions

1. According to Acts 18, how long did Paul minister at Corinth?

2. Describe the make-up of the converts in Corinth.

3. How can converts from such diverse and immoral backgrounds ever come into unity?

4. Is the presence of supernatural spiritual gifts to be considered as evidence of spiritual maturity? Give evidence to support your answer from scripture, observation, and personal experience.

5. If the Corinthian church walked in the description of love as defined in 1 Corinthians 13:4-8, how many of its problems would continue to exist?

6. Take the agape love test. Before each description of a characteristic of love, insert your name in the space provided:

   a. _____ suffers long
   b. _____ is kind
   c. _____ does not envy
   d. _____ is not puffed-up
   e. _____ is not provoked
   f. _____ endures all things

How true is this description? Are you rejoicing or repenting?

Chapter Nine

Love	Longsuffering	Faith
Joy	Gentleness	Meekness
Peace	Goodness	Temperance

Joy, Praise, and Hope

*"These things I have spoken to you, that **My joy** may remain in you, and that **your joy** may be full." (John 15:11)*

*"Most assuredly, I say to you that you will weep and lament, but the world will rejoice; and you will be sorrowful, but your sorrow will be turned into **joy**. A woman, when she is in labor, has sorrow because her hour has come; but as soon as she has given birth to the child, she no longer remembers the anguish, for **joy** that a human being has been born into the world. Therefore you now have sorrow; but I will see you again and your heart will rejoice, and your **joy** no one will take from you. And in that day you will ask me nothing. Most assuredly, I say to you, whatever you ask the Father in My name He will give you. Until now you have asked nothing in My name. Ask, and you will receive, that your **joy** may be full." (John 16:20-24)*

The early church was full of joy. This was the evidence that the first believers were full of the Holy Spirit. Jesus promised that no man could take their joy from them. Indeed, in spite of all the opposition they faced, they were full of joy. Luke, the author of Acts, declares, *"The disciples were filled with joy and the Holy Spirit."* (Acts 13:52)

John the Beloved spread joy as he preached and wrote (1 John 1:4; 2 John 12).

Jesus was a man of joy. He was not a solemn, downcast man that never smiled. As awful as the cross was, He went to it with joy, fulfilling the Father's will, and for our sake (Heb. 12:2). The joy the disciples experienced was His joy (John 15:11), shared with them. Swarms of children flocked around Jesus. Would they have been drawn to a solemn man? He spread joy wherever He went. His miracles left people rejoicing. He was anointed with the oil of gladness (Heb. 1:9).

Jesus trusted His Father, and had boundless hope for the future. He was doing His Father's will and worked with a sense of God's approval on His life. Knowing He was providing a great service for the people produced an inner joy that carried Him through the difficult times.

There is joy in heaven. The angels rejoice over every sinner that repents (Luke 15:3-10). God Himself rejoices over us with singing (Zeph. 3:17)! Indeed, in His presence is fullness of joy (Ps. 16:11).

The New Testament demonstrates the overwhelming joy of the early church. Let us look at a few of the references to joy and take note of the kind of joy the early church experienced. In believing, they were filled with **all joy** (Rom. 15:13). The preaching of the gospel brought **great joy** to the hearers (Acts 8:8; 15:3; Luke 24:52). Even through times of great trial and deep poverty, they were carried by an **abundance of joy** (2 Cor. 8:2). In the midst of affliction, they received the word with the **joy of the Holy Spirit** (1 Thess. 1:6). Peter said they rejoiced with **joy inexpressible and full of glory** (1 Pet. 1:8). In spite of difficulties, their **joy was exceeding** (Jude 24; 1 Pet. 4:12-13; Matt. 5:12).

Indeed, joy characterized the experience of the early church. Heavy opposition, trials, and threatening circumstances could not dampen life in the Spirit. The triumphant testimony of the Book of Acts bears witness to this fact. The converts on the Day of Pentecost ate their bread with gladness (Acts 2:46). The apostles were filled with an overcoming attitude (Acts 4:20). Miracles were continuous (Acts 5:12-16). They rejoiced that they were counted worthy to suffer for the name of Jesus (Acts 5:40-42). The spreading of the gospel brought great joy (Acts 8:8). Conversion left the Ethiopian eunuch rejoicing (Acts 8:39). Miraculous answers to prayer brought exciting gladness (Acts 12:14). Even when they were expelled out of cities, they were absurdly joyful in the Holy Spirit (Acts 13:52). The Philippian jailer was brought into joy (Acts 16:34). Though bonds and affliction awaited Paul in all his journeys, he went through them all with joy (Acts 20:24).

The Spirit-filled life is mighty and the joy of the Lord overcomes all outer circumstances. The Spirit of God cannot be held down. This understanding of God and the joy He provides persuaded Paul that nothing would be able to separate him from the love of God, which is in Christ Jesus. In all these things, he is more than a conqueror:

*"Yet in all these things we are **more than conquerors** through Him who loved us. For I am persuaded that neither death nor life, nor angels nor principalities nor powers, nor things present nor things to come, nor height nor depth, **nor any other created thing, shall be able to separate us from the love of God which is in Christ Jesus our Lord."** (Rom. 8: 37-39)*

What a man of God! Does it appear that Paul was fully persuaded of God's love? Does it seem that Paul was full of the joy that Jesus possessed – the kind that Peter declared was "inexpressible and full of glory?"

The Lord foretold that His followers would have great trials in this world, but in the midst of it, they would be sustained with great joy that the world could not take away from them. Obviously, then, this joy is not found in human strength. It is not to be confused with the world's concept of happiness. Happiness is dependent upon circumstances (happenings). When surroundings are pleasant to one's momentary taste and preference, one will be happy. The joy of the Lord is different; it is resident in the Holy Spirit (1 Thess. 1:6; Rom. 14:17). Therefore, it does not need to draw upon the comforts or dictates of this world.

For instance, let us consider the hometown crowd at a sports event. Have you ever noticed how quickly the noise from the exuberant crowd diminishes when an opposition player scores? The chants change from cheers to jeers! The happiness of the crowd depends to a large extent upon the scoreboard. If the home team is winning the game, the crowd is hilariously happy and noisy. When the scoreboard numbers are reversed, it becomes depressed and relatively silent. Definitely happiness is dependent upon circumstances.

Now, contrast the previous example with the following illustration of joy found in Exodus 15.

After the Lord miraculously parted the waters of the Red Sea, and their triumphal passage on dry land was completed, Moses and the children of Israel, obviously filled with joy, burst into singing that famous song known as *The Song of Moses*. While this never-to-be-forgotten experience was a circumstance in their lives, it was a manifestation of the love and power of God. The true joy produced in their hearts could not be contained and they entered into praise – singing *The Song of Moses*. Miriam and the women, finding singing insufficient release of their joy, took timbrels and danced before the Lord. Indeed, joy is resident in God Himself (Ex. 15:20-21).

Jesus promised His disciples three things: they would be in constant trouble; they would be fearlessly courageous; and they would be absurdly joyful. He promised a joy that would carry them through anything. As Nehemiah had said, the joy of the Lord is the strength of the believer (Neh. 8:10). Though the Hebrew believers were made gazingstocks by reproaches and afflictions, and though their goods were confiscated, they had the untouchable joy of the Lord that was unmoved by adverse circumstances (Heb. 10:33-34). God produces an exuberant joy that the world knows nothing about. Believers do not need to seek this world's happiness; they possess something far superior; they have the joy of the Lord.

The gospel is the proclamation of glad tidings (Acts 13:32; Luke 8:1; Rom. 10:15). It leaves joy with those who receive it. It convicts men of sin, but it does not leave them in that state. It forgives them, and gives them an overcoming life, free from the burdens that have weighed them down. The gospel heals the sick, brings peace, and can be received by all who believe.

This overcoming joy that we have been discussing encourages faith, and betrays itself by praise. The garment of praise has replaced the spirit of heaviness (Isa 61:3). The joy of the Lord is normal, and praise unconsciously escapes the lips of the redeemed.

There are times when a believer may be tempted to take his eyes off the Lord and place them on circumstances. In such times, the believer needs to be reminded that the Lord is the source of his joy. Believers are to encourage each other in the joy of the Lord. Titus was an encouragement to Paul (2 Cor. 7:13). Paul helped the Corinthians in their joy (2 Cor. 1:24). Peter wrote his first epistle to cheer up the discouraged believers (1 Pet. 1:3-9; 4:12-14).

The prophet Joel spoke of a time when joy was withered away from the sons of men. Joy and gladness were cut off from the house of God (Joel 1:12-16). However, the pouring out of the Spirit would bring joy back into the hearts of men (Joel 2:18-32). The Psalmist had lost his joy, and was downcast in soul. He would command his soul to hope again in God, and approach God who was his exceeding joy (Ps. 42, 43).

After the initial experience of joy, it is the perspective of hope that preserves it. Hope relates to the future (Rom. 8:24-25). At the present, the church awaits the hope of righteousness (Gal. 5:5). Irrespective of what is transpiring at the moment, God is moving toward a definite end. Christ is returning, and salvation will be consummated at the resurrection. The believer is to rejoice in hope of the glory of God (Rom. 5:2; Ps 16:9-11). God will fulfill all His promises. This expectation fills the believer with joy.

The writer of Hebrews exhorts his readers to know the full assurance of hope unto the end (Heb. 6:11). The believer is to allow hope to act as a magnet to which all the faculties of his soul will be attracted and focused. The mind, will, emotions, and conscience are to be governed by the goal of the Christian faith, not by things as they appear at the moment. In this way, hope acts as an anchor to the soul (Heb. 6:19).

Since hope is the expectancy of the fulfillment of these promises, those who possess hope have a joyful anticipation of good. It is a favorable and confident expectation and is the opposite of worry and anxiety. Those with hope display a cheerful mind and have an optimistic approach to life irrespective of the circumstances. In Paul's list of the Christian armor in 1 Thessalonians, he refers to the helmet of the hope of salvation (1 Thess. 5:8). God is the author of hope (Rom. 15:13).

Although a specific word from God may not be received in a given situation, we can place confidence in God. We can trust His character because we know that He is good. The Psalms are replete with examples of confident hope in times of adversity. It is this hope in God that helps our joy. The soul learns to rejoice in God and His goodness, giving birth to the expression of joy: praise!

Believers filled with the full assurance of hope have learned to praise and to "enter" the joy of the Lord (c.f. Matt. 25:21,23). Certainly, we have great role models to follow: Old Testament prophets such as Habakkuk and New Testament believers like the Apostle Paul. They knew that in difficult surroundings, they could and should rejoice in the Lord. Hear Habakkuk's heart in the following:

*"Though the fig tree may not blossom, Nor fruit be on the vines; Though the labor of the olive may fail, And the fields yield no food; Though the flock may be cut off from the fold, And there be no herd in the stalls – **Yet I will rejoice in the Lord, I will joy in the God of my salvation.** The Lord God is my strength; He will make my feet like deer's feet, And He will make me walk on my high hills."* *(Hab. 3:17-19)*

Another excellent example of praise in the Old Testament is the story of King Jehoshaphat in 2 Chronicles 20. In the face of overwhelming odds, the nation of Judah made a decision not to be governed by fear of their enemies. Instead, they would rejoice and praise in the very face of danger! When they praised, God sent ambushments against their enemies. They did not need to fight the battle, but they did collect the spoils! Hallelujah!

Perhaps one of the most outstanding examples of joy in the New Testament is that of Paul during his Roman imprisonment. The epistle to the Philippians reveals his joyful frame of mind in spite of all the negative factors working against him. In this letter to the saints at Philippi, the words "joy" and "rejoice" are found many times.

Paul's enemies had accused him falsely, causing his imprisonment that could lead to his execution. However, his joy in the Lord remained untouched. As he prayed for others, he was filled with thankfulness and confidence, and the element of joy pervaded his requests:

*"I thank my God upon every remembrance of you, always in every prayer of mine **making request for you all with joy,** for your fellowship in the gospel from the first day until now, being confident of this very thing, that He*

who has begun a good work in you will complete it until
the day of Jesus Christ;" (Phil. 1:3 -6)

Rather than allowing a negative attitude toward his circumstances to spoil his joy, he viewed them as a way by which the
proclamation of the gospel increased:

> *"But I want you to know, brethren, that the things which*
> *happened to me have actually turned out for the **further-***
> ***ance of the gospel,** so that it has become evident to the*
> *whole palace guard, and to all the rest, that **my chains***
> ***are in Christ;** and most of the brethren in the Lord, hav-*
> *ing become confident by my chains, are much more bold*
> *to speak the word without fear. ... What then? Only that*
> *in every way, whether in pretense or in truth, Christ is*
> *preached; And in this **I rejoice, yes and will rejoice.***"
> *(Phil. 1:12-14, 18)*

With respect to his upcoming trial that could result in his execution, Paul's soul was free from all concerns, showing instead
confidence and joy (Phil. 1:19-26). If he were to be executed, he
said it would be his joy to lay down his life in the service of others' faith (Phil. 2:16-18).

Paul exhorts his readers to continue in the joy of the Lord, for
that is the Christian life (Phil. 3:1-3; 4:4). Whatever the circumstances around us, our confidence is to be in the Lord who gives
joy in the midst of it all. This, the world cannot comprehend, nor
take away!

The fruit of the Spirit is joy. The Christian joys in the salvation
of his God. He has been delivered from a miserable existence,
and anticipates the glorious consummation of his salvation at the

return of Christ. From beginning to end, the joy of the Lord is indeed his strength!

Conversion ———————————————▶ **Future Hope**

Gospel of
Glad Tidings
brings initial joy

Continuous attitude of
joyous anticipation!

Thought Questions

1. How could a man such as Paul be joyful even in death?

2. What adjectives does the New Testament employ to describe the believers' experience of joy?

3. What is the difference between happiness and joy?

4. How does the New Testament describe a believer's initial joy at his conversion?

5. How can we encourage one another and ourselves in the joy of the Lord?

6. How does praise relate to joy?

7. How does hope relate to joy?

8. Relate an incident from your own life that reveals how the joy of the Lord brought you through to victory. How did you encourage yourself?

Chapter 10

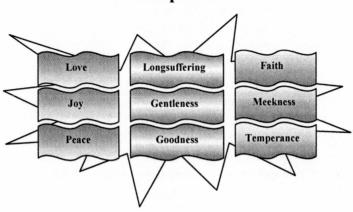

Peace

> *"Now may the **God of peace** who brought up our Lord Jesus Christ from the dead, that great Shepherd of the sheep, through the blood of the everlasting covenant, make you complete in every good work to do His will, working in you what is well pleasing in His sight, through Jesus Christ, to whom be glory forever and ever. Amen." (Heb. 13:20, 21)*

Frequently in the New Testament, God is referred to as the *"God of peace"* (Phil. 4:9; Rom. 15:33; 16:20; 1Thess. 5:23). Paul declared that God is not the author of confusion, but of peace (1 Cor. 14:33).

One of the titles of Christ is the *"Prince of Peace"* (Isa. 9:6). The coming of Christ was to guide our feet into the way of peace (Luke 1:79). Indeed when Christ was born, the angels announced to the shepherds that there was to be peace on earth (Luke 2:14).

Peace is a fruit of the Spirit. As with joy, its source is not in this world, but in the Spirit of God (Rom. 14:17). It is the peace of Christ Himself (John 14:27).

The New Testament word for peace contains the idea of "rest" and "quietness." The New Testament concept of peace arises from its Old Testament roots, where the Hebrew word is "shalom." This is a very general word, and gives the idea of "safety," "completion," "friendliness," and "to reciprocate." The root of this word (shalom) is used extensively in Exodus 22, and has heavy usage meaning the reconciliation of differing parties. It is translated in such terms as "make amends," "recompense," "render," "requite," and "reward."

Out of this term came the familiar greeting "shalom." It is most often translated as "peace," and is a wish that all is well, that the individual is not in trouble, nor has any reason to be troubled. Shalom can be translated as "favor," "friend," "greet," "health," "prosper," "rest," " safe," " salute," "welfare," and "well." All of these concepts are brought forward to the New Testament.

The wish of peace is characteristic of the New Testament. Almost all of the epistles begin their salutation with a pronouncement of peace. Often Jesus would say *"Go in peace"* after working a healing. When taking leave of someone, a Hebrew would say *"Peace be with you."* (c.f. Judges 6:23; Dan. 10:19; Matt. 10:13). To experience peace is to come into harmony and right relationships.

Peace with God

*"Therefore, having been justified by faith, **we have peace with God through our Lord Jesus Christ**," (Rom. 5:1)*

*"and by Him to reconcile all things to Himself, by Him,
whether things on earth or things in heaven, **having
made peace** through the blood of His cross. And you,
who once were alienated and enemies in your mind by
wicked works, yet now He has reconciled in the body of
His flesh through death, to present you holy, and blame-
less, and above reproach in His sight-" (Col. 1:20-22)*

The gospel of Jesus Christ brings peace with God. The atonement has reconciled those who were once enemies of God. All
barriers between God and the human race have been removed by
the shedding of the blood of Jesus Christ. Those who by faith
trust and rely upon Christ are thus brought into harmony with
God. Assurance fills the heart, and there is no fear of the wrath
of God. The believer experiences tranquility while waiting for
the return of Christ (2 Pet. 3:13-14). The gospel is the gospel of
peace (Acts 10:36; Eph. 6:15).

Peace of God

*"These things I have spoken to you, that **in Me you may
have peace.** In the world you will have tribulation; but
be of good cheer, I have overcome the world." (John
16:33)*

No matter what the outer circumstances may be, the believer
remains undisturbed. The peace Christ brings to the heart of man
is humanly impossible to imitate. Paul expounds on this peace in
Phil. 4:6-9. It passes all understanding and keeps the heart and
mind. The peace of God protects the mind and heart from the
harmful effects of worry and anxiety. This calm delight, like joy,
comes by believing God (Rom. 15:13). Peace with God has led
to knowing the peace of God in the heart. Abiding in the proper
relationship with the Lord perpetuates this wonderful fruit of the

Spirit. He whose mind is stayed on the Lord, trusting Him, will know perfect peace (Isa. 26:3). To be spiritually minded is life and peace (Rom. 8:6).

Peace with One Another

Unity in the Body of Christ, comprised of members with many differing backgrounds and cultures, is only possible because of the fruit of the Spirit – the development of love. A study of passages such as Eph. 4:1-7, Col. 3:12-17, and Rom. 13-16 will reveal this fact. Meekness, longsuffering, love, peace, goodness, gentleness are all mentioned in these passages that deal with the oneness of the Body of Christ. In particular, Paul, when using the analogy of the human body to describe the church, speaks of two "bonds" or "bands" that hold the members in correct relationship (c.f. Col. 2:19). They are bonds of love (Col. 3:14) and peace (Eph. 4:3). In exhorting the Corinthians to be of one mind and to live in peace, Paul makes it known that it is the God of love and peace that makes it possible (2 Cor. 13:11). Love and peace are the bands that hold the body of Christ together. A band refers to the ligaments that hold the bones together, making "joints" possible. A joint is a place of fellowship.

Peace with God and the peace of God, like all other phases of the Christian life, should naturally spill over into our relationships with one another. If they do not, then our experience with God is far more mental assent than it is heart change. John very plainly states that a person who claims to love God, but does not love his brother, is a liar (1 John 4:20-21). *"If it is possible, as much as depends on you, live peaceably with all men." (Rom. 12:18) "Pursue peace with all people, and holiness, without which no one will see the Lord:" (Heb. 12:14)*

The presence of the Holy Spirit is required to make this a reality. People who happen to believe the same thing may have friendships, but not necessarily achieve biblical unity. Even sinners can get along quite well (Luke 6:32-34). The Spirit of God unites people of differing backgrounds into the one Body of Christ. We are never told in scripture to create unity. We are united by virtue of the fact that we have been made to drink of the same Spirit (1 Cor. 12:13). Our common experience of receiving the Spirit baptizes us all into the Body of Christ. Thus the Spirit creates the Body; it is not our creation. The Spirit creates the fellowship Christians enjoy one with another (Phil. 2:1). This being the case, unity in the Body is maintained and sustained by life in the Spirit, and by no other means. This is why Paul exhorts us to keep, not create, *"the unity of the Spirit in the bond of peace." (Eph. 4:3)*

Within the unity of the Body of Christ, there is a wide diversity of gifts and divine enablements (Rom. 12:3-8). Different anointings, styles, and mannerisms abound. Dissimilar temperaments tend to see any situation from different perspectives. The scripture makes it plain that we need one another, and that we will become all God intends us to be through our relationships one with another. The flesh of man would allow these differences to be points of division, but by the Spirit of God they become opportunities for complementing one another. We are responsible for each other's edification (c.f. 2 Cor. 10:8; 13:10).

In light of this, we are commanded to actively seek peace in our relationships with one another. God is very interested in reconciling people! The disciples had been arguing among themselves about who should be the greatest. Jesus, in Mark 9:50, states that they should *"have salt in yourselves, and have peace with one another."* Every sacrifice was to be salted. By this He meant for them to keep pureness in heart and motive, denying jealousy and

bitterness a foothold in their lives. The disciple of Christ is responsible to watch over his attitudes.

Peace is to be actively pursued. We are responsible to seek it,
and not just allow it to happen. At all times, by following after
the things that make for peace, we must insure peace in the
Body of Christ.

> *"Therefore let us **pursue the things which make for
> peace** and the things by which one may edify another."
> (Rom. 14:19)*

> *"Flee also youthful lusts; but **pursue** righteousness,
> faith, love, peace with those who call on the Lord out of
> a pure heart." (2 Tim. 2:22)*

> *"and to esteem them very highly in love for their work's
> sake. **Be at peace** among yourselves." (1 Thess. 5:13)*

> *"Let him turn away from evil and do good; Let him **seek
> peace and pursue it**." (1 Pet. 3:11)*

We are to be peacemakers (Matt. 5:9) by consciously exerting
an effort to bring peace and a sense of rest into our relationships,
instead of strife and tension. James states that the fruit of righteousness is sown in peace of them that make peace (James
3:18). He is addressing a situation that is gendering strife and
confusion. What is the meaning of his statement? The seed contains the fruit. Peace is the seed; righteousness in our lives is the
fruit, the harvest. Therefore, those who seek, follow, and make
peace foster righteousness toward one another, and facilitate the
church's growth, development, and fruitfulness.

Peacemakers have a positive attitude toward those who oppose them; they overcome evil with good (Rom. 12: 18-21). Peacemakers love their enemies, bless those who curse them, do good to those who hate them, and pray for those who spitefully use them and persecute them (Matt. 5:38-45). Blessed are the peacemakers, for they shall be called the sons of God (Matt. 5:9).

Thought Questions

1. Explain in your own words the progression from peace with God, to peace of God, to peace with others.

2. What concepts are meant by the Hebrew word "shalom?"

3. Is our attitude toward peace to be passive or are we to actively to pursue it? Give an application from your own life.

4. Why do you think peacemakers are called the sons of God?

Chapter Eleven

Longsuffering, Gentleness, Goodness

Longsuffering

Longsuffering begins the second trio of fruit (longsuffering, gentleness, goodness) that deals specifically with our relationships with one another. The first trio of fruit (love, joy, peace) describes our relationship to God, which then creates the atmosphere for relationships with each other. By receiving the same Spirit, and by our common experience of love, joy, and peace, we are brought into alliance with one another.

The first cluster of fruit has been quite enjoyable. Love, joy, and peace – what more could a person desire or need! Do we really need the relationships with each other that are mentioned in this next trio of fruit (longsuffering, gentleness, goodness)? Apparently the Lord thinks so, because now our experience of God will be tested and proved in our associations with one another. We are now moving from bearing fruit to bringing forth more fruit (John 15:2). In this verse, Jesus clearly states that pruning or purging produces greater fruit bearing. No wonder then that longsuffering starts this second trio of fruit! In Paul's beautiful description of love to the troubled Corinthian church, he mentions longsuffering as the first characteristic they needed to acquire (1 Cor. 13:4).

In modern English, the words "patience" and "longsuffering" are often considered to be synonymous. These words are somewhat similar, but certainly not identical in meaning. The difference in meaning needs to be appreciated to fully understand the fruit of longsuffering. A study of these words found in the following scriptures will help prepare us for the definitions provided below (Col. 1:11; 2 Cor. 6:4, 6; 2 Tim. 3:10).

Patience undergirds faith, so that it neither surrenders to circumstances nor crumbles under trial. It is the opposite of despondency and cowardice and is linked to hope. Patience gives us the ability to remain firm when our faith is tried; it causes us to continue in faith when outer pressures tempt us to quit. Patience has the effect of changing our character and breaking us of our self-sufficiency (1 Pet. 1:9).

> *"My brethren, count it all joy when you fall into various trials, knowing that the testing of your faith produces **patience**. But let patience have its perfect work, that you may be perfect and complete, lacking nothing." (James 1:2-4)*

> *"And not only that, but we also glory in tribulations, knowing that tribulation produces **perseverance**; and perseverance, character; and character, hope." (Rom. 5:3-4)*

Longsuffering is like patience, except it generally, but not always deals with our relationships with one another. It is the quality of self-restraint in the face of provocation that does not hastily retaliate or promptly punish. It is the opposite of wrath, revenge, anger, and is linked to mercy. Longsuffering describes the man who can hold back anger rather than yield to it. It is the control of negative factors.

> *"A wrathful man stirs up strife, But he who **is slow to anger** allays contention." (Pro. 15:18)*

> *"He who **is slow to anger** is better than the mighty, And he who rules his spirit than he who takes a city." (Pro. 16:32)*

> *"The discretion of a man makes him **slow to anger**, And his glory is to overlook a transgression." (Pro. 19:11)*

Longsuffering produces forbearance. Those who are longsuffering forbear others (Eph. 4:2; Rom. 2:4).

> *"Therefore, as the elect of God, holy and beloved, put on tender mercies, kindness, humility, meekness, **longsuffering**; bearing with one another, and forgiving one another, if anyone has a complaint against another; even as Christ forgave you, so you also must do." (Col. 3:12-13)*

Longsuffering means to be patient with one another. It is the forbearance that endures evil deeds and injuries without being provoked to anger or revenge. There are many scriptures that state this is how the Lord acted toward a hostile world. Paul's testimony shows that God was longsuffering toward him during his persecution of the church:

*"However, for this reason I obtained mercy, that in me first Jesus Christ might show **all longsuffering**, as a pattern to those who are going to believe on Him for everlasting life." (1 Tim. 1:16)*

The Lord is long suffering toward the world, for He is not willing that any should perish, and His longsuffering provides salvation for many:

*"The Lord is not slack concerning His promise, as some count slackness, but is **longsuffering toward us**, not willing that any should perish but that all should come to repentance." (2 Pet. 3:9)*

*"and consider that the **longsuffering of our Lord is salvation** – as also our beloved brother Paul, according to the wisdom given to him, has written to you." (2 Pet. 3:15)*

Forbearance means to hold up, to hold one's self erect and firm, to sustain one's self, or to tolerate. When this term is used of God, it refers to a delay of punishment (Rom. 2:4; 3:25).

Obviously then, we can assume that in the Body of Christ there will be considerable opportunity for irritation. The fruit of long-suffering enables us to control our anger and hold in check our reactions. A paraphrase of Proverbs 19:11 could read: **Longsuffering is the basis of a forgiving spirit.** If the fruit of longsuffering defers our anger, then forgiveness is possible. This is exactly what Paul teaches in Col. 3:12-13. When the fruit of long-suffering is present, forbearance follows, allowing one to forgive rather than to enter into a quarrel. This heals relationships. Nobody wants to be around an angry person who overreacts to the slightest stimulus. We are commanded to put away anger (Eph. 4:31). Anger rests in the bosom of fools (Eccl. 7:9).

Longsuffering is a necessity for the development of Christian maturity. Paul continually met with opposition from others (2 Cor. 6:6; 2 Tim. 3:10). The minister of the gospel must have longsuffering if he is to be used of God to touch others' lives (2 Tim. 2:24-25). Christ Himself was longsuffering with His disciples. He said to them in Mark 9:19, *"How long shall I bear with you?"* How often did Jesus show longsuffering when his disciples failed to comprehend what He taught, or argued and disputed among themselves? How many arguments must have transpired between Matthew, a former tax collector, and Simon the Zealot, who was taught to hate such men?

Longsuffering is not an option for our lives; it is a necessary part of our development. God intends to unite us with those who don't see as we see. Iron sharpens iron, and God will bring two seemingly opposing attitudes into a position of complementing one another. Therefore, we are commanded to be patient with all men (1 Thess. 5:14).

Gentleness

It is a matter of history that the heathen (Gentiles) frequently confused the two Greek words: Chrestos and Christos. The former is translated as gentleness or kindness, the latter as Christ. These Greek words are used together in 1 Pet. 2:3: *"if indeed you have tasted that the **Lord is gracious**."* The heathen described the Christian as either Chrestos or Christos. May that testimony be repeated today!

Galatians 5:22 is the only place in the King James Version of the scripture that "chrestos" is translated as "gentleness." More frequently and accurately, it is rendered as "kindness." In some places, chrestos is translated as "goodness," "better," "easy," or **"gracious."**

It is highly significant that kindness often follows longsuffering, as it does in the passage where the list of the fruit of the Spirit is given (Gal. 5:22-23). In 1 Cor. 13, a very familiar portion of scripture, Paul shows that love is longsuffering, and then kind (1 Cor. 13:4). Paul was approved as a minister of God by both longsuffering and kindness (2 Cor. 6:6).

Longsuffering is the Holy Spirit's ability to control negative factors in our lives, such as anger. If we are longsuffering with one another in the Body of Christ, we will not seek revenge. However, the Holy Spirit desires to accomplish more than longsuffering in our lives. We must learn to be kind to those who provoke us. Longsuffering passively endures; kindness actively confers blessing.

Kindness describes family relationships. The English word "kindness" is possibly derived from "kindred." We have been "kin-ned" together as the family of God, and thus treat one another as family. Kindness is descriptive of the relationships and attitudes family members should exhibit toward one another.

Kindness, or gentleness, is a moral excellence of character that may be described, in part, as follows:

- o Showing yourself useful and serviceable
- o Sweetness of temper that puts others at ease
- o Kindly disposition shown in active service
- o Opposite of severity (Rom. 11:22)
- o Mild in opposition to harshness, maliciousness, sharpness, bitterness (Eph. 4:31 –32)

o Opposite of burdensome (Matt. 11:30)
o Never producing dissention in other people
o Characteristic of strength
o Not burly or boastful
o Not defensive or retaliative

Three fruit of the Spirit reflect the character of God Himself, which is produced in believers by the Holy Spirit. Both King David, the psalmist of Israel, and the prophet Isaiah recognized this fact:

*"You have also given me the shield of Your salvation; Your **gentleness** has made me great." (2 Sam. 22:36)*

*"Oh, give thanks to the Lord, for he is **good!** For His mercy endures forever." (Ps. 106:1; Ps. 107:1)*

*"I will mention the lovingkindness of the Lord And the praises of the Lord, According to all that the Lord has bestowed on us, And the **goodness** toward the house of Israel, Which He has bestowed on them according to His mercies, According to the multitude of His **lovingkindnesses." (Isa. 63:7)***

The kindness of God follows His longsuffering. His longsuffering defers His anger, and He reaches out to us in kindness, working for our benefit. Nehemiah, rehearsing the history of the children of Israel, declared that God, even when provoked, was slow to anger, and of great kindness (Neh. 9:17). The prophet Joel exhorted his hearers to turn to the Lord, appealing to the same attributes:

"So rend your heart, and not your garments; Return to the Lord your God, For He is gracious and merciful, **Slow to anger, and of great kindness** *... ." (Joel 2:13)*

Jonah's displeasure concerning God's dealing with the wicked city of Nineveh was based on his knowledge that God would be slow to anger (longsuffering) and then of great kindness:

"So he prayed to the Lord, and said, 'Ah, Lord, was not this what I said when I was still in my country? Therefore I fled previously to Tarshish; for I know that You are a gracious and merciful God, **slow to anger** *and abundant in* **lovingkindness***, One who relents from doing harm.' " (Jonah 4:2)*

God is kind even to the unthankful and evil (Luke 6:35). It is because of the kindness of God that we are saved (Eph. 2:7). God's kindness went beyond His longsuffering of our behavior. Not only did he forbear our sins committed against Him, but also He actively pursued our benefit and good.

The Holy Spirit develops this same kindness (gentleness) in us, and we direct it toward others. In the context of not grieving the Holy Spirit, we are instructed to put away all bitterness, wrath, clamor, evil speaking, and malice. Instead, we are admonished to be kind, tenderhearted, and forgiving one another, for this is how God, for Christ's sake, has forgiven us (Eph. 4:30-32).

When we are kind and tenderhearted, we enable forgiveness to restore a wrongdoer into right relationship so that love removes the wrong. In other words, kindness understands the feelings of others, considers those feelings, and adapts its attitudes, words, and behavior accordingly. A believer who is not governed by the Holy Spirit will resort to harsh or sharp criticism, and make verbal attacks on the offender. However, the Holy Spirit desires to work into us the qualities of gentleness and mercy.

In Col. 3:12-13, Paul mentions some of the fruit of the Spirit and their effects toward others: kindness is coupled with mercies; meekness is demonstrated toward others as humbleness of mind; longsuffering is recognized by forbearance of one another. The fruit of kindness in us will be made visible to others by mercy demonstrated. Kindness, born within by the Holy Spirit, leads to compassion, pity, mercy, and sympathy for another, even when that other person has offended us in some way.

It is very interesting to note that mercy, which is the outcome of kindness, is included in some of the greetings in Paul's epistles. When writing to individuals, Paul added mercy to grace and peace in his salutation (1 Tim. 1:2; 2 Tim. 1:2; Tit. 1:4), whereas only grace and peace are mentioned when writing to a corporate church (Col. 1:2; Phil. 1:2; Eph. 1:2). This serves to underscore that the second trio of fruit (longsuffering, gentleness, and goodness) describes our relationships with one another. Long-suffering withholds anger and retaliation when provoked; gentleness is a sweet disposition to the wrongdoer, and leads to goodness, which brings benefit to the offender.

Goodness

Goodness is the natural progression in the development of the nature of Christ in the believer by the Holy Spirit. It follows after longsuffering and gentleness. Longsuffering passively endures any evil done against it, holding in check any passions of the mind before it acts. Gentleness (kindness) is the spirit in which the believer responds, returning blessing for evil, actively doing good. Notice the directive given by Paul regarding the diffusing of negative situations:

*"Beloved, do not avenge yourselves, but rather give place to wrath; for it is written, 'Vengeance is Mine, I will repay,' says the Lord. Therefore 'If your enemy is hungry, feed him; If he is thirsty, give him a drink; For in so doing you will heap coals of fire on his head.' Do not be overcome by evil, but **overcome evil with good.**" (Rom. 12:19-21)*

Goodness, practical piety, is mentioned frequently in the New Testament. Its primary meaning refers to being good in constitution and character. Good things are brought out of the good treasure of a good man's heart (Matt. 12:35). Goodness brings profit and benefit to others. It is expressed by well doing, and is recognized by generosity and benevolence.

Some religious people of Jesus' day considered themselves good because they did not engage in certain sins and vices; others acquired their goodness by the keeping of rules. Jesus openly opposed such a false notion. Goodness is more than just the opposite of a negative quality.

Goodness is a grace, a compassionate yearning and tenderness toward others, that prods us into action. Goodness sees a need, encourages and stands by the needy one, and irrespective of the inconvenience, seeks to bring benefit.

The term "good" is derived from the Anglo-Saxon word "god." "Good" is simply an expansion of "God." To be filled with goodness is to be Godlike in our thoughts and actions. Goodness consists in loving people, helping them become better persons, meeting their needs, and bringing edification to them. Goodness is kindness that performs; it is mercy that moves.

There are many examples of goodness in action throughout scripture:

*"how God anointed Jesus of Nazareth with the Holy Spirit and power, who went about doing **good** and healing all who were oppressed by the devil, for God was with Him." (Acts 10:38)*

*"Then He said to them, 'Is it lawful on the Sabbath to do **good** or evil, to save life or to kill?' But they kept silent. And when He had looked around at them with anger, being grieved by the hardness of their hearts, He said to the man, 'Stretch out your hand.' And he stretched it out, and his hand was restored as whole as the other." (Mark 3:4,5)*

"Then Jesus answered and said, 'A certain man went down from Jerusalem to Jericho, and fell among thieves, who stripped him of his clothing, wounded him, and departed, leaving him half dead.

"Now by chance a certain priest came down the road. And when he saw him, he passed by on the other side.

"Likewise a Levite, when he arrived at the place, came and looked, and passed by on the other side.

*"But a certain Samaritan, as he journeyed, came where he was. And when he saw him, he had **compassion**. So he went to him and bandaged his wounds, pouring on oil and wine; and he set him on his own animal, brought him to an inn, and took care of him. On the next day, when he departed, he took out two denarii, gave them to the innkeeper, and said to him, 'Take care of him; and*

*whatever more you spend, when I come again, I will re-
pay you.'*

*"So which of these three do you think was neighbor to
him who fell among the thieves?" And he said, "He who
showed mercy on him." Then Jesus said to him, "Go and
do likewise." (Luke 10:30-37)*

Dorcas made coats and garments, and was spoken of as full of
good works and almsdeeds – charitable giving (Acts 9:36, 39).
This was love in action. Cornelius obtained a good report among
the Jews for his almsgiving (Acts 10:1-2,22). Joseph of Ari-
mathaea, being a good man, gave Jesus a dignified burial place
(Luke 23:50-53).

Good works are the product of the fruit of goodness. The scripture is replete with exhortations to do good works as evidence of
the work of God in our lives. The grace of God abounds toward
us so that we may have abundance for every good work (2 Cor.
9:8). We are to do good to all men as we have opportunity (Gal.
6:10). Good works are so important that God has ordained that
we should walk in them and they are the end purpose of His
working in us (Eph. 2:10). To walk worthy of the Lord is to be
fruitful in every good work (Col. 1:10). The end of the Lord's
dealing with us is to establish us in every good work (2 Thess.
2:15-17). Patient continuance in well doing is the mark of those
who prepare themselves for judgment and its rewards (Rom.
2:7). The pastoral epistles (1 Timothy, 2 Timothy, and Titus) are
full of exhortation to do good works. Good works are the evidence of a changed heart!

Good works give testimony before the world. Heathens will be
convinced of the reality of the claims of the gospel because they
see the fruit of goodness producing good works. This will turn
their false accusations about us to their salvation:

*"having your conduct honorable among the Gentiles, that when they speak against you as evildoers, they may, **by your good works** which they observe, **glorify God in the day of visitation.**" (1 Pet. 2:12)*

It is by good works that the church shines as a light to the world, bringing the gospel to the needy and praise to God (Matt. 5:14-16).

Paul states that it is the fruit of the Spirit that distinguishes the children of light from the children of darkness. In viewing the fruit of the Spirit from this angle, the difference is summed up as goodness, righteousness, and truth:

*"For you were once darkness, but now you are light in the Lord. Walk as children of light (for the fruit of the Spirit is in all **goodness, righteousness, and truth**), finding out what is acceptable to the Lord. And have no fellowship with the unfruitful works of darkness, but rather expose them." (Eph. 5:8-11)*

The works of darkness are unfruitful, yielding no benefit. Life in the Spirit is fruitful, and proves itself beneficial. Goodness refers to the disposition that leads to good works. Righteousness refers to integrity, careful attention against disorder and injustice, rendering to all their dues. Finally, the fruit of the Spirit holds high regard for truth, believing it, reverencing it, speaking it, hoping and rejoicing in it.

Goodness is the spontaneous reaction of the heart to a need, and doesn't require an outward organization of programs before it acts. Do we need to be told to care for others? Doesn't the Holy Spirit convict us of that? The aim of God is to make us perfect unto every good work to do His will. This perfection is the result of the working of God in us (Heb. 13:21).

The fruit of goodness is needed in the Body of Christ. Believers are held together in unity by goodness and the other fruit of the Spirit. Every one of us is to please his neighbor for his edification. Being filled with goodness, we are able to admonish one another (Rom. 15:2,14).

Perhaps the story of Barnabas is the best example of the fruit of goodness in the believer's life. Because of the goodness of Barnabas, both Paul and Mark became fruitful ministers of the gospel of Jesus Christ. For this reason, the next chapter will focus entirely on Barnabas, a good man.

Thought Questions

1. Generally speaking what is the difference between long-suffering and patience?

2. What is a good paraphrase of Proverbs 19:11?

3. Is there is a person in your life with whom you must suffer long? Do you view this as an opportunity to develop fruit?

4. In your own words describe the biblical fruit of kindness.

5. Why does longsuffering always precede kindness?

6. Why does goodness follow kindness?

7. Read the short epistle to Titus and comment on Paul's remarks about good works.

8. Explain how this trio of longsuffering, gentleness, and goodness affect the daily life of the church. Give examples from your relationships to other members of the Body of Christ.

Chapter Twelve

Barnabas – A Good Man

*"Then news of these things came to the ears of the church in Jerusalem, and they sent out Barnabas to go as far as Antioch. When he came and had seen the grace of God, he was glad, and encouraged them all that with purpose of heart they should continue with the Lord. **For he was a good man, full of the Holy Spirit and of faith.** And a great many people were added to the Lord." (Acts 11:22-24)*

"And Joses, who was also named Barnabas by the apostles (which is translated Son of Encouragement), a Levite of the country of Cyprus," (Acts 4:36)

Barnabas is an excellent illustration of a person who exemplifies the fruit of goodness. As seen in Acts 4:36, his original name was Joses, but he was renamed Barnabas by the apostles. This was in accordance with his character, for his ministry was one of comfort and encouragement.

Goodness means practical piety. While gentleness, the fruit preceding goodness in Paul's famous list (Gal. 5:22-23), is an inward disposition that shows itself actively doing good, goodness is the natural outflow from it. As Matthew 12:35 shows, goodness primarily means to be good in character and constitution, and is beneficial in its effects. As will be demonstrated through the life of Barnabas, a good person brings profit and benefit to others. Goodness is expressed in well doing.

Barnabas' life exemplified this wonderful grace of goodness. Never passive, he was prodded into action by a compassionate yearning and tenderness toward others. When he saw a need, he acted on it. Being an encourager, he stood with people and wasn't dissuaded by the inconvenience. The **Son of Encouragement** exhibited a kindness that performed, a mercy that moved, and a caring that did not consider the cost.

When first mentioned in scripture (Acts 4:36-37), Barnabas was already known for his grace. Although from the priestly tribe of Levi, he was an early convert to Christ. Filled with the Holy Spirit, he participated in the joy of the Lord. His love and joy seemed boundless as he sold land and gave the profits to help the needy of the church.

Since Barnabas and Saul of Tarsus ministered together for a considerable period of time, we need to get some background information on Saul, who later became known as Apostle Paul.

Saul was a sworn enemy of the fledgling church, tirelessly persecuting it. When Ananias first received instructions from the Lord to visit and pray with Saul (Acts 9: 10-19), he hesitated because of Saul's reputation as a dangerous enemy of the church. The Lord encouraged Ananias with this declaration found in Acts 9:15-16, *"Go, for he is a chosen vessel of Mine to*

bear My name before Gentiles, kings, and the children of Israel.
For I will show him how many things he must suffer for My
name's sake."

After Saul's conversion, he remained certain days at Damascus
with the disciples, who were amazed at the thoroughness of the
change that had taken place in his heart.

Soon Saul's former associates became his enemies, as he was
now powerfully and aggressively preaching the faith that he
once tried to destroy (Gal. 1:23). A plot to capture and kill Saul
was thwarted when the disciples lowered him down the wall of
the city, facilitating his escape from the garrison intent on si-
lencing him (Acts 9:23-25; 2 Cor. 11:32-33).

Having fled from Damascus, Saul went to Jerusalem, the city
that witnessed the beginning of the persecution. The cruel op-
pression of Christians there had included the martyrdom of
Stephen, a believer full of faith and power, one who had done
great wonders and signs among the people (Acts 6:8). Saul had
been present at the stoning of this precious saint and took great
pleasure in his death:

> *"But he, being full of the Holy Spirit, gazed into heaven*
> *and saw the glory of God, and Jesus standing at the right*
> *hand of God, and said, 'Look! I see the heavens opened*
> *and the Son of Man standing at the right hand of God!'*
> *Then they cried out with a loud voice, stopped their ears,*
> *and ran at him with one accord; and they cast him out of*
> *the city and stoned him.* **And the witnesses laid down**
> **their clothes at the feet of a young man named Saul.***"*
> *(Acts 7:55-58)*

Stephen's martyrdom spurred the young and zealous Pharisee to reverse the situation described in this verse:

> *"Then the **word of God spread**, and the **number of disciples multiplied greatly** in Jerusalem, and a **great many of the priests were obedient to the faith.**" (Acts 6:7)*

Saul, a member of the strictest sect of the Pharisees, had taken great pride in his Jewish heritage (Acts 26:4-5; Phil. 3:4-6). As the most promising young man in the Pharisaic traditions, Saul commenced doing whatever he could to defame the name of Jesus of Nazareth and to decimate His followers. He put many saints into prison, and promoted their execution. He punished them in every synagogue and compelled them to blaspheme. Being exceedingly enraged, he chased them even to foreign cities, until his conversion on the road to Damascus (Acts 26:9-18).

It is no surprise that the apostles at Jerusalem did not willingly receive Saul. They were all afraid of him. Not certain that he was truly a disciple, they probably wondered whether this was a trick aimed at obtaining more information about the believers in the church. Understandably, they were cautious, as this man was responsible for the imprisonment and death of many believers in the city. Jerusalem had widows and orphans because of Saul's actions against them.

> *"But Barnabas took him and brought him to the apostles. And he declared to them how **he had seen the Lord** on the road, and that **He had spoken to him**, and how **he had preached boldly at Damascus in the name of Jesus.**" (Acts 9:27)*

At this point Barnabas came to Saul's rescue. Risking his own reputation, and unconcerned about the cost, Barnabas believed in and saw the potential of a former enemy of the church. Mercy reached past the hurt that Saul had caused, and looked at the heart of the man. Perhaps Barnabas discerned that Saul had acted in ignorance and unbelief (1 Tim. 1:13), and that he was really fighting the conviction incurred by hearing the preaching of Stephen (Acts 7:2-53).

Being a good man, and ever willing to comfort and to bring out the best in people, Barnabas befriended the former adversary. Having taken him into his confidence, he then became the young convert's spokesman. He was able to convince the apostles of the genuineness of Saul's miraculous conversion. Through the persuasion of Barnabas, Saul was admitted into the fellowship of the church he had tried to destroy. Saul went in and out of Jerusalem with the apostles and spoke boldly in the name of the Lord Jesus. **What a marvelous testimony of the grace of goodness, bringing reconciliation, trust, and forgiveness into such a difficult and tension filled situation!**

At Jerusalem, attempts on Saul's life occurred and he had to flee again. The brethren sent him to the safety of his hometown, Tarsus (Acts 9:30). There he remained for sometime in obscurity.

One of the results of the persecution that started with the stoning of Stephen was the spreading of the gospel outside of Jerusalem. As people fearing for their lives fled the city, the word began to be proclaimed throughout Judea and Samaria, as the Lord originally intended:

*"But you shall receive power when the Holy Spirit has come upon you; and **you shall be witnesses to Me in Jerusalem, and in all Judea and Samaria, and to the ends of the earth.** " (Acts 1:8)*

While many believers still were governed by some of their tradi-
tional thought, there were some from Cyprus (Barnabas' homeland) and Cyrene that spoke beyond the normal boundaries of
Judaism as they preached to the Grecians. A great number of
Gentiles were converted at Antioch (Acts 11:19-21). This presented problems for the Jewish mind. Now, the Holy Spirit had
moved outside their normally accepted perimeters. What would
they do with Gentiles who were not circumcised and knew nothing of the laws of Moses?

This was a difficult question. The conversion of a Gentile named
Cornelius had already stirred much excitement and debate.
Change was taking place, and this situation had to be handled
with great care. How could the church accept the uncircumcised
Gentiles without offending the Jews? A man of understanding,
gentleness, and compassion was needed to investigate this com-
plication. He must be free from prejudice and have a heart large
enough to embrace all whom God was bringing into the church.
The delegate the church would send to Antioch would have to
be a man full of the Holy Spirit and faith, and endowed with the
right disposition and character traits. The man they chose was
Barnabas, a good man (Acts 11:22-24).

Barnabas was well received by the Gentile saints at Antioch. He
quickly admonished them to cleave to the Lord. However,
Barnabas recalled the teaching ability of Saul of Tarsus who had
gone into obscurity in his hometown in Cilicia. Ever willing to
promote another, Barnabas embarked on a journey to Tarsus to
persuade him to minister in this new Gentile church. The beginning of a partnership that lasted many years occurred when
Barnabas and Saul returned to Antioch together.

Because of Barnabas' thoughtfulness and consideration, Saul
was given an opportunity to share the things that the Holy Spirit

had taught him. The former terrorist and opponent of the gospel of Jesus Christ now had a platform to share his teaching in a setting not threatening to him. After a year of their teaching at Antioch, free from the legalizing influence of the Judaizers, the saints became known as Christians. Certainly, his association with Barnabas, known for his goodness, gave Saul his beginning in ministry.

Some prophets from Jerusalem came to Antioch and signified by the Spirit that a famine would come throughout the world. The church determined, as every man was able, to prepare and send relief to their fellow believers in Judea. The relief was sent to the elders in Judea by the hands of Barnabas and Saul. This act of benevolence was very typical of Barnabas, and probably it gave the idea to Saul. Later, Paul, as he was called then, attempted to build a bridge between the Jewish church and the Gentile churches by encouraging the Gentile saints to send an offering to their Jewish brethren in need (1 Cor. 16:1-4; 2 Cor. 8:1-5; Rom. 15:31).

Saul and Barnabas were sent together by the Holy Spirit on a mission trip, where Saul was noted as the principal speaker, and became the more famous personality:

> *"Now in the church that was at Antioch there were certain prophets and teachers: Barnabas, ... , and Saul. As they ministered to the Lord and fasted, The Holy Spirit said, 'Now separate to Me Barnabas and Saul for the work to which I have called them.' Then, having fasted and prayed, and laid hands on them, they sent them away. So, being sent out by the Holy Spirit, they went down to Seleucia, and from there they sailed to Cyprus. And when they arrived in Salamis, they preached the*

word of God in the synagogues of the Jews. **They also had John as their assistant.** *(Acts 13:1-5)*

This trip, which began in Barnabas' homeland – Cyprus, saw many converts and miraculous events. Upon their return to Antioch, they testified that God had opened the door of faith to the Gentiles, as He had done with them at Antioch (Acts 13 & 14). Paul and Barnabas remained in Antioch, teaching and preaching the word of the Lord.

After some time, Paul and Barnabas expressed a desire to revisit the churches started during their first journey. A disagreement occurred between them. The difference of opinion centered on a young man named **John Mark, better known as Mark** (who later wrote the gospel that bears his name).

Mark was related to Barnabas (Col. 4:10). On their first journey together, Mark went with them as a helper (Acts 13:5). For reasons unknown, Mark left the two apostles at Pamphilia, and journeyed back home to Jerusalem.

Barnabas, desiring to restore and rebuild Mark, wanted to take him on the second journey. Paul disagreed because Mark had already demonstrated his inability to make the trip. This disagreement became so sharp that Paul and Barnabas separated and made journeys in opposite directions. Paul chose Silas as his traveling companion; Barnabas took Mark under his care.

Although at this point Barnabas faded into history, his influence did not. Years later, Paul spoke well of Barnabas (1 Cor. 9:6). The fruit of Barnabas' merciful and helpful disposition benefited Paul throughout the remainder of his life. Later on, Mark became a part of Paul's apostolic team and was one of Paul's fellow laborers (Philemon 23-24). He was present with Paul when the apostle was in prison. Paul had given specific instructions concerning the church's responsibility to receive Mark (Col. 4:10). Just prior to his execution at the hands of the Romans, Paul instructed Timothy to bring Mark, for he was profitable and useful to Paul in the ministry (2 Tim. 4:11).

Once again, **the goodness of Barnabas prevailed and wrought a great victory.** Mark was lifted up in spite of previous failure, and restored to usefulness in the kingdom of God. Mark also became a close companion of Peter, who referred to him as his son (1 Pet 5:13). Peter went to Mark's house in Jerusalem when he was so miraculously delivered from prison and execution (Acts 12:12). Mark, the coworker, friend, and companion of both Paul and Peter authored *The Gospel According to Mark.*

Through Barnabas, the lesson of goodness is abundantly exemplified. Goodness fosters the victory that comes by believing in others, building up others, and standing with others. Thanks to the goodness of this one man, the Gentile church received its foundation and obeyed the command to go into the entire world with the gospel of Jesus Christ. Because of the love of this outstanding individual, Paul became not only one of the great teachers but also one of the great apostles of the early church. Perhaps, without the kindness of Barnabas, many of the epistles that comprise so much of the New Testament would be absent. Without the mercy of Barnabas, Mark, a profitable servant of the Lord, may not have completed his ministry.

The story of Barnabas is proof that Christian character has a great deal to do with the success of the gospel of Jesus Christ. Undoubtedly, many surprises will become evident at the judgment seat of Christ, when countless unseen acts of kindness will receive their rewards in that day. **Barnabas was a good man!**

Thought Questions

1. How do you think Barnabas influenced Saul of Tarsus?

2. Is it possible that Mark would have left the ministry if it were not for Barnabas?

3. Why was Barnabas the correct choice to send to the Gentile converts in Antioch? How important was the trait of goodness found in Barnabas to that situation?

4. In what way is the fruit of goodness evident in your own life? How do you encourage others?

Chapter Thirteen

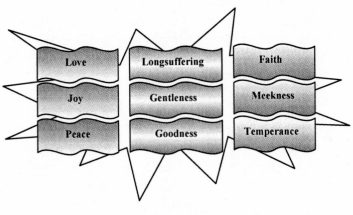

Faith

*"Now faith is the substance of things **hoped** for, the evidence of things **not seen**." (Heb. 11:1)*

Concerning the list of the fruit of the Spirit in Gal. 5:22-23, many of the modern day versions of scripture render the seventh fruit as "faithfulness" while the others retain the root "faith." The Greek word is definitely just the root "faith." Understandably, anyone who stands in faith will continue to be faithful where he stands. Faith is the force, action, and cause; faithfulness is the flow, reaction, and effect.

Earlier in our study, we saw that the fruit of the Spirit is the expansion, development, and maturing of love from the famous triad of faith, hope, and love. In love, God speaks a word to us; the fulfillment of that word is our hope; and hope gives birth to faith in the present. **Faith is the convictive persuasion that it shall be as God has said, and will persevere through the present waiting period.** Between the time that God speaks a word (imparting faith) and the time it is fulfilled (our hope), our faith will be tested, sometimes over many years. In the meantime, our faith refashions our minds, wills, emotions, and consciences. Many doubts, and battles of discouragement, disillusionment and fear will be waged as God produces the nature of love in us, which is then described more fully as the fruit of the Spirit (Gal. 5:22-23).

Three trios may be noticed in the list of the fruit of the Spirit. The first trio describes our initial reaction to God (love, joy, peace). These virtues naturally spill over to love for others (longsuffering, gentleness, goodness), and finally produces complete control of self (faith, meekness, temperance).

How is it that faith belongs to the overarching trio of faith, hope, and love, and appears again in the third trio of the fruit of the Spirit? This indicates that faith has a progressive persuasion over our lives.

Pure love for God and others develops as we die to ourselves. The self-life must be dealt with, so God permits the trying of our faith:

> *"In this you greatly rejoice, though now for a little while, if need be, you have been grieved by various trials, that the genuineness of your faith, being much more precious than gold that perishes, though it is tested by fire, may be found to praise, honor, and glory at the revelation of Jesus Christ, whom having not seen you love. Though now you do not see Him, yet believing, **you rejoice with joy inexpressible and full of glory, receiving the end of your faith – the salvation of your souls.**"*
> *(1 Pet. 1:6-9)*

The phrase "salvation of your soul" does not refer to a person's conversion experience, but to the continuing and progressive reformation of character. Faith, as a fruit of the Spirit, will trust in God, hold fast to Him, and have confidence in Him. When things around us are shaken, faith holds us secure to God.

The third trio of fruit leads progressively to conquering the dictates of self. When the process is finished, the power of sin will be completely undone. Faith makes room for meekness, which in turn leads to temperance, or the control of self. Love for God leads to love for others, which brings complete submission of the self-life to the Holy Spirit.

Meekness is the attitude that accepts the dealings of God as good, so that we become "better" instead of "bitter." The testing of our faith (fruit of the Spirit) is once again a pruning in our lives for greater fruitfulness. Faith acts as an anchor to our souls so that we don't fall away in the times of adversity that God has allowed for our good. We learn meekness through confidence and trust in the character of God; then meekness lends its energy for self-control.

Jesus spoke of bearing fruit, more fruit, and much fruit (John 15:2,5). The Father is glorified when we bear much fruit (John 15:8); and that occurs when we have learned faith, meekness, and temperance. Jesus explained that a grain of wheat must fall into the ground and die if it is to bear "much" fruit:

> *"Most assuredly, I say to you, unless a grain of wheat falls into the ground and dies, it remains alone;* ***but if it dies, it produces much grain.*** *He who loves his life will lose it, and he who hates his life in this world will keep it for eternal life." (John 12:24-25)*

Jesus then explained that the bearing of much fruit requires dying to life in this world and finding true spiritual life.

It is possible to have self at the center of our love for God and others. We can be self-righteous, self-centered, and self-sufficient. We may be dependent on our emotions, feelings and reasoning for our sense of spirituality. We may be lazy in our wills, or stubborn in ourselves. There may be many areas of our lives that are not broken of an independent attitude.

The self-will needs to be broken. Often, to touch these "inward" attitudes, God must allow some "outer" circumstances to be touched. We will find ourselves in adverse situations over which we have no control. Sometimes even the sense of God's presence seems afar off. Prayer may be hard, and the sweetness is gone. A stripping is taking place. Our faith is under trial and God is often silent during these difficult circumstances. We ask for His guidance and a response is not forthcoming.

The fruit of faith must bring us to a place of trust and surrender. Faith will cause us to trust God when reasoning fails. We trust God in spite of our lack of emotion. Inwardly, we are fighting for a conviction that God really is in control, and that He knows what He is doing. In times like this, we must trust solely in the character of God, even in the absence of any word from Him. Without explanation, we must come to the conclusion that He knows what is best. We trust Him because we know that He is good, truthful, and powerful. Faith always translates into our lives as trust and obedience. The "Hall of Faith" (Heb. 11) records the lives and examples of many men and women of faith. Yet their stories told in the Old Testament (KJV) never mention the word "faith." They are only recorded as people who trusted and obeyed. Apostle Paul understood this in his own experience, and showed that he was brought to a place where he could not trust in himself for deliverance, but in God who raises the dead (2 Cor. 1:9-10). In one of Job's better moments, he spoke of the testing of his faith (Job 23:8-9), and showed its anchor (23:10), its boldness (23:11-12), its knowledge (23:13-14), its fear (23:15-17) and its marvel (24:1).

To trust, as it is revealed throughout scripture, means: to roll our needs upon God, and then to wait patiently for Him to act; to run to God and His promises for refuge when doubt and fear plague us; to confide in God as our trusted friend, and to lean on Him as our strongest supporter; and to hope when things seem hopeless.

In times of trial, instead of falling away we remain obedient to God. The fruit of faith becomes the principle that controls and guides us, and by which we live the Christian life.

Thought Questions

1. How do faith and faithfulness relate to each other?

2. The fruit of faith introduces the third trio of fruit. In which direction does this fruit grow?

3. Do you agree that it is possible to still have self at the center of your love for God and others? Why or why not?

4. What two words does the Old Testament constantly use to describe what the New Testament calls faith?

5. Using the definition of the word "trust" as given in this chapter, relate an incident or experience from your life that demonstrates this trust. How could you have trusted God more fully?

Chapter Fourteen

Meekness

To fully convey the meaning of the word "meekness" in a few words is extremely difficult, perhaps impossible. Consequently, we shall devote this chapter to a somewhat lengthy discussion of this fruit of the Spirit.

The world incorrectly defines meekness as equivalent to weakness, cowardliness, spinelessness, or faintheartedness. By this definition, a person is meek if he is incapable of helping himself or unable to face life's problems, and passively surrenders to every obstacle. This statement is completely false!

Meekness, the fruit of power, is an inwrought grace of the soul resulting from the dealings of God. It is a quality of the inner man that accepts the dealings of God as good, and therefore receives them without disputing, murmuring, sulking, or resisting. Meekness manifests itself as a complete surrender to God's will and displays no sign of the independent self-life.

We are to *"receive with meekness the implanted word, which is able to save our souls (James 1:21).* It is the humble (meek) He guides in justice and teaches His way (Ps. 25:9). Thus a person who is meek will be teachable, tractable, and moldable.

God allows insults and injuries to inflict His people for chastening and purifying purposes. He, in an indirect way, is dealing with us through these secondary agents. Thus, we should not see the hand of men as abusive; we must see the hand of God at work preparing us for glory. We perceive the hand of God bringing needed correction, and consequently, we are meek before men. Submission to God will result in courtesy to others, even to those who bring affliction. James 4:7 states, *"Therefore submit to God. Resist the devil and he will flee from you."*

Meekness is closely associated with humility and lowliness. The inner grace of meekness appears before men as humility. A meek person is not boisterous (Eph. 4:2). In the context of Col. 3:12-15, meekness and humbleness of mind will show a delicate consideration for the rights and feelings of others, especially when rebuking or disciplining. Meekness is amazed at the mercy God has shown and the great debt of sin He has forgiven. Therefore meekness deals with other offenders gently:

> *"Brethren, if a man is overtaken in any trespass, you who are spiritual* **restore such a one in a spirit of gentleness***, considering yourself lest you also be tempted."* *(Gal. 6:1)*

> *"***in humility*** correcting those who are in opposition, if God perhaps will grant them repentance, so that they may know the truth,"* *(2 Tim. 2:25)*

When Jesus told the multitudes to learn of Him, He brought attention to His meekness and lowliness:

*"Come to Me, all you who labor and are heavy laden, and I will give you rest. Take My yoke upon you and learn from Me, for **I am gentle and lowly in heart**, And you will find rest for your souls." (Matt. 11:28-29)*

Jesus was meek, not because He was weak, but because He had the infinite resources of heaven at His command. Meekness is the opposite of self-assertiveness and self-interest. It is neither elated nor cast down because it is not occupied with self. If Jesus had chosen to exhibit it, He had plenty of authority to assert Himself!

A meek person sees the need for change within himself, and knows both the mercy of God and his own sinful passions at the same time. When trials and adverse circumstances come, he will allow himself to be dealt with and become better instead of bitter. This attitude grows in strength and is not capable of weakness. Meekness is the fruit of power. Strength of character is needed to submit to the hand of God, and not retaliate against the people who injure. Moses was the meekest man on the face of the earth (Num. 12:3). He endured many complaints against him and did not retaliate, but rather went to God, allowing God to search him more deeply.

Meekness draws its strength from understanding two basic facts: God loves us and we love God. This confidence allows us to build meekness. No matter how threatening the circumstance, we cannot deny the love in our heart for God. Since God is love, all that God permits is for our good:

*"And **we know that all things work together for good** to those who love God, to those who are the called according to His purpose." (Rom. 8:28)*

Meekness is strength under control. It can be likened to a person who possesses tremendous wealth and power, and at the same time, uses compassion, courtesy, and consideration for the best interests of those less powerful. It is also like a person with great muscular strength who applies himself to a delicate task with the utmost care.

A most excellent example of meekness is found in the life of Joseph as related in the book of Genesis. Joseph held the power to do whatever he wished to his evil brothers, who had sold him into slavery decades earlier. Joseph had learned that God used all the insults and injuries he received in the early years of his life to direct him into the position he now enjoyed:

> *"But now,* ***do not therefore be grieved or angry with yourselves because you sold me here; for God sent me before you to preserve life.*** *For these two years the fam-ine has been in the land, and there are still five years in which there will be neither plowing nor harvesting. And God sent me before you to preserve a posterity for you in the earth, and to save your lives in a great deliverance. So now it was not you who sent me here, but God; and He has made me a father to Pharaoh, and lord of all his house, and a ruler throughout all the land of Egypt."* (Gen. 45:5-8)

When Joseph had the opportunity to retaliate, he responded with kindness and blessing, saving the very ones who were cruel to him. Indeed, Joseph was a meek man.

Obviously, meekness is not a natural characteristic of people. It is a fruit of the Spirit, and is the result of the Holy Spirit's influ-ence upon the hearts of men. Our energies are trained to serve the will of another, not our own will. Meekness requires the breaking of the independent self-life.

The Greek word that was translated as meekness was used to describe an animal that had been trained and domesticated by its master. For instance, a wild horse needs to be broken of its wild and independent nature so that it can run a race, or be used for pleasure riding. A trained horse will pick up the slightest signal from its rider and instinctively obey. As a horse is being trained, it learns meekness. God would have us serve His will and purposes, not our own independence and self-will. As in the illustration of the horse, it is strength under control. Our lives are to come under the control of the Holy Spirit. Meekness is power.

Self-love puts high value on self-assertiveness. The world continually beckons us to strike it rich and be successful! As we become broken, we gain a willingness to leave everything - our rights, our past, our future. We come to the point that all we want to possess is God Himself. Nothing else matters; there is no need to defend our dignity. There is a confidence that God is in control, and that heaven and earth belong to Him. The meek have the promise that they shall inherit the earth (Ps. 37:11; Matt. 5:5), and that promise is sufficient. The meek are joint-heirs with Christ, and will reign with Him. Knowing this, the meek have no need to assert themselves to climb the ladder of success. The worldly try to "possess" by accumulating huge bank accounts and owning vast territories of land, but they will leave it all behind! The world cannot see eternal realities. Those in the world need to dominate others for a sense of power that they cannot take beyond the grave.

By contrast, the meek can suffer unjustly without retaliating when others abuse and injure them in the pursuit of power and prestige. They know God loves them and will vindicate them righteously. The meek will be saved at the day of judgment (Ps. 76:9). The wicked will be cast down to the ground, but the meek will be lifted up (Ps. 147:6). The meek are beautified with salvation (Ps. 149:4).

Therefore, with this view, there is no need to slay our rivals, but rather our self-centeredness. Jesus, in His unjust sufferings, simply committed all to Him that judges all things righteously:

> *"For this is commendable, if **because of conscience toward God one endures grief, suffering wrongfully.** For what credit is it if, when you are beaten for your faults, you take it patiently? But when you do good and suffer, if you take it patiently, this is commendable before God. For to this you were called, because Christ also suffered for us, leaving us an example, that we should follow His steps: 'Who committed no sin, Nor was deceit found in His mouth'; who, **when He was reviled, did not revile in return; when He suffered, He did not threaten, but committed Himself to Him who judges righteously;"** (1 Pet. 2:19-23)*

The world, since it does not have an eternal view, sees meekness as worthless. However, the world and its form are fading away (1 Cor. 7:31). The world cannot see the tremendous power and strength of the meek, or the power of humility. When we have meekness, we can treat all men with courtesy; we can rebuke without rancor; we can argue without intolerance; we can face the truth without resentment; we can be angry and not sin; and we can be gentle but not weak.

Here, randomly listed in point form, are a few thoughts regarding meekness, some of which have been stated previously:

1. Moral power is greater than brute force. Gentleness may be forced to yield to brute force at times, but the victory of brute force is short-lived.

2. God wants us to learn meekness (Matt. 11:29; 2 Cor. 10:1).

3. Seek and follow after meekness (Zeph. 2:3; 1 Tim. 6:11).

4. The triumph of gentleness, courtesy, kindness and love is enduring.

5. Jesus rode into Jerusalem on a donkey, meekly (Matt. 21:5).

6. Meekness wins victories that force cannot obtain.

7. We triumph through humility.

8. Some signs of meekness are approachability, sensitivity to the spirits of others, teachability.

9. Meekness is to be shown toward all men (Tit. 3:2).

10. Meekness is characteristic of the true wisdom from above (James 3:13).

11. Pride and arrogance will weaken spiritual life.

12. Meekness will seek the spiritual good of its opponents.

13. The meek, like Jesus, are restful for they will be satisfied (Ps. 22:26) and inherit the earth (Ps. 37:11).

14. The meek have no driving need to dominate others to prove themselves.

15. Meekness is a humble submission to the teachings of divine revelation.

16. God places a higher value on meekness than on gold (1 Pet. 3:3-4).

Thought Questions

1. What is the world's understanding of meekness?

2. A meek person is described as teachable, tractable, and moldable. What do these words mean?

3. Are you able to see the hand of God behind the many difficult circumstances of life? Are you allowing the hardness in your heart to be broken or do you resist?

4. How does a meek person bring correction to others?

5. Meekness is strength under control. What do you think this means?

6. How is a wild animal domesticated?

7. Why does meekness follow after the fruit of faith?

8. Attempt to describe the fruit of meekness in your own words.

Chapter Fifteen

Temperance

Modern English uses the word "temperance" almost exclusively for abstinence from intoxicating drinks. However, this is not the biblical meaning of the word. Temperance, often called self-control, may be defined as self-restraint in conduct, expression, and indulgence of appetites.

We are now being brought to the goal of the Holy Spirit's influence in our lives. The full and complete exchange of our lives for the life of Christ is the final outworking of the fruit of the Spirit. God has not given us a spirit of fear, but He has given us the Spirit of power that leads us through love into the development of a sound mind:

> *"For God has not given us a spirit of **fear**, but of **power** and of **love** and of a **sound mind**." (2 Tim. 1:7)*

Love develops and blossoms, causing us to respond to God in love, and to love others as Christ loved us. The self-life dwin-

dles away under the control of love. Self-control now binds all
the fruit into one glorious harmony.

Self is the origin of all sin. Adam chose to act independently of
God when he partook of the fruit from the tree of the knowledge
of good and evil. He then obtained knowledge apart from a relationship with God, thus promoting his self-life. Through disobedience to God, sin entered into Adam's life and into ours. Now,
the development of the fruit of the Spirit in our lives is the undoing of the self-life. The manifestation of the life of Christ, typi-
fied by the tree of life, fills our lives in the absence of self.

Temperance is achieved when good self-government controls
our appetites. God bestowed great powers, desires, abilities and
drives in mankind. When governed properly, these faculties
serve good and beneficial purposes, bringing increasing joy to
our lives. Their proper use demands the controlling power of the
will under the operation of the Spirit of God. However, when
out of control, after enslaving us, they bring destruction. This is
true of any capability we have, whether it is in the realm of emotions, passions, or physical needs and drives. There may be
many outside enemies whose attacks we can withstand, but a
single enemy from within our passions can cause us to fall.
Lack of self-control simply delivers authority over to all the enemies without! For instance, people who cannot control anger are
defenseless against their enemies (Prov. 16:32; 25:28). Without
good government chaos reigns and liberty is a figment of the
imagination. Liberty must serve a purpose; otherwise, it will
degenerate into self-serving bondage. It should never provide an
occasion for serving the flesh:

> *"For you, brethren, have been called to **liberty**; only do
> not use liberty as an opportunity for the flesh, but
> through love serve one another." (Gal. 5:13)*

We must submit all our God-given faculties to Him for His purposes; then, they will be given direction through a sense of purpose under God:

*"Therefore, whether you eat or drink, or whatever you do, **do all to the glory of God.** " (1 Cor. 10:31)*

The history of the Israelites is replete with illustrations of the need to pass over the reins of their lives to God. After liberation from their enemies by the power of God through anointed judges, the Israelites returned repeatedly to their own ways, bringing bondage back upon themselves (Judges 2:16-23). Perhaps, from the stories concerning their "taking their eyes off God," we can glean imperative direction for our lives.

We can all think of situations when, having passed our stress levels, we have thrown caution to the wind, and thought, said, or done regretful things. Authority can be abused in the home, church or place of vocation. Appetite gone awry becomes an addiction. That control is an absolute necessity for productivity should be obvious. Anything out of control will not yield fruitfulness.

For instance, fire can give heat for warmth and cooking, but out of control it is very destructive, quickly causing untold damage. Water gives moisture for crops and quenches thirst, but a flood brings devastation. Cars transport us anywhere there are roads, but if they are pushed beyond our abilities to control them and negotiate the roads, they become deadly weapons in our hands.

A revealing example of the grave danger of not developing the fruit of temperance is found in the story of Samson, as recorded in Judges 13-16. Though he was anointed with great power, his lack of self-control led him to an early and cruel death.

Samson was chosen of God for a special mission. He was the last of the great judges to bring deliverance to Israel. His exploits were many. Single-handedly, he frustrated the Philistines again and again. Once, he captured three hundred foxes, tied torches to their tails and released them through the crops of the Philistines. On another occasion, he killed a thousand Philistines with nothing but the jawbone of a donkey. On another occasion, he lifted the gates of the city, along with its anchoring posts, and carried them uphill on his back!

Unfortunately, Samson chose to lead a life unshackled by restraints. His parents had no power to dissuade him from marrying a Philistine girl, even though this action was contrary to the law of God. Even a lion in the way did not deter Samson from his erroneous behavior. He used the supernatural charismatic ability God had given him to destroy the warning God had sent him!

Samson continually violated the Nazarite vow that was upon his life. He touched dead animals, walked through vineyards, and visited prostitutes! He allowed lust, anger, and desire for revenge to develop unbridled in his life.

Samson came to a tragic end. His choice of intemperance cost him his eyes, his dignity, and ultimately his life. Even in his death, he did not deliver Israel. He only defeated the Philistine leaders. His call to ministry suffered, falling short of God's intended purposes.

The story of Samson should serve as a powerful reminder of the absolute necessity for character development in the lives of God's people. Samson lacked self-control, which beautifully binds all the fruit into a harmonious and complete unity.

Lack of self-control is inherent in the nature of the world, and contributes to the perilous times of the last days (2 Tim. 3:3). In general, the world is intemperate regarding anything it pursues – money, pleasure, and appetites. Jesus accused the Pharisees of His day of being intemperate (no self-control), and full of extortion and excess:

> *"Woe to you, scribes and Pharisees, hypocrites! For you cleanse the outside of the cup and dish, but inside they are full of extortion and **self-indulgence**. Blind Pharisees, first cleanse the inside of the cup and dish, that the outside of them may be clean also." (Matt. 23:25-26)*

In other words, the Pharisees possessed things acquired by violence, and used them without any self-control. Paul gave advice to those who had strong sexual desires:

> *"Do not deprive one another except with consent for a time, that you may give yourselves to fasting and prayer; and come together again so that Satan does not tempt you because of your lack of **self-control**." (1 Cor: 7:5)*

> *"but if they cannot exercise **self-control**, let them marry. For it is better to marry than to burn with passion." (1 Cor. 7:9)*

Intemperance means lack of strength, want of self-control, and powerlessness. The fruit of the Spirit called temperance in Gal. 5:23 stands in contrast to the many works of the flesh mentioned previously in Galatians: fornication, uncleanness, lustfulness, drunkenness and reproach (Gal. 5:19-21).

In his day, Peter needed to resist false teaching that actually encouraged intemperance. In the teaching being presented, liberty appeared to be equivalent to serving self-interests. In his second epistle, Peter showed the pathway to true knowledge of God:

> *"But also for this very reason, giving all diligence, add to your faith virtue, to virtue knowledge, **to knowledge self-control**, to self-control perseverance, to perseverance godliness, to godliness brotherly kindness, and to brotherly kindness love. For if these things are yours and abound, you will be neither barren nor unfruitful in the knowledge of our Lord Jesus Christ." (2 Pet. 1:5-8)*

Notice the sequence in the development of love, starting with faith. The fact that temperance follows knowledge suggests that we have to practice the knowledge we have gleaned from the scriptures. True knowledge leads to self-control, not away from it. It brings perfect freedom found only in God's service, not false liberty produced by the doctrine of those teachers. Their teaching offers a temptation that would bind their followers. Temperance leads to patience and patience leads to godliness. Godliness signifies the submission of our wills to God.

Temperance is required for the office of bishop (or pastor):

> *"For a bishop must be blameless, as a steward of God, not self-willed, not quick-tempered, not given to wine, not violent, not greedy for money, but hospitable, a lover of what is good, sober-minded, just, holy, **self-controlled**," (Tit. 1:7-8)*

Christians face many difficulties concerning temperance. Some have no control over their thoughts or anger. Yet the biblical command is not to sin in our anger (Eph. 4:26). There is a proper use of anger that can be a bulwark to the soul. Note the use of righteous anger in the following verses from scripture:

*"Then He went into the temple and began **to drive out those who bought and sold in it**, saying to them, 'It is written, My house is a house of prayer, but you have made it a den of thieves.' " (Luke 19:45-46)*

*"And He entered the synagogue again, and a man was there who had a withered hand. So they watched Him closely, whether He would heal him on the Sabbath, so they might accuse Him. And He said to the man who had the withered hand, 'Step forward.' Then He said to them, 'Is it lawful on the Sabbath to do good or to do evil, to save life or to kill?' But they kept silent. And when **He had looked around at them in anger, being grieved by the hardness of their hearts**, He said to the man, 'Stretch out your hand.' And he stretched it out, and his hand was restored as whole as the other." (Mark 3: 1-5)*

Jesus was zealous for the work of His Father and He showed righteous anger when an intentional hindrance was placed in His path. Unfortunately, our anger too often is not righteous, nor zealous for the cause of God.

The scripture reveals that the greatest evidence of intemperance is committed with the tongue, that tiny but unruly organ:

*"But **no man can tame the tongue**. It is an unruly evil, full of deadly poison. With it we bless our God and Father, and with it we curse men, who have been made in the similitude of God. Out of the same mouth proceed blessing and cursing. My brethren, these things ought not to be so." (James 3:8-10)*

The greatest area of nonconformity to the Spirit, and stressed in the New Testament, involves the sins of the tongue. The tongue reveals the condition of the heart, for out of the heart the mouth speaks (Matt. 12:34-35). Scripture has much to say about gossip, rumors, exaggeration, lies, sarcasm, accusations, criticisms, corrupt communications, foolish jestings, evil speaking, clamoring, and such things. The epistle of James devotes considerable space to this topic (James 3:2-12). Paul also recorded the fact that the sins of speech are the most common way of grieving the Spirit, and destroying His work (Eph. 4:25-32).

At the judgment to come, temperance will be seen as the causative factor in our gaining the reward. While in prison, Paul reasoned with Felix about righteousness, temperance, and judgment (Acts 24:25). Righteousness speaks of God's claims, and temperance speaks of man's response to those claims. Judgment will determine the extent to which man has exercised the proper self-government to follow those claims. Temperance now is the vitally important issue as we prepare for the judgment to come.

Let us liken the Christian life to a race, using the analogy supplied in Hebrews and 1 Corinthians:

> *"Therefore we also, since we are surrounded by so great a cloud of witnesses, let us lay aside every weight, and the sin which so easily ensnares us, and let us run **with endurance** the race that is set before us,"* (Heb. 12:1-2)

> *"Do you not know that those who run in a race all run, but one receives the prize? Run in such a way that you may obtain it. And everyone who competes for the prize is **temperate** in all things. Now they do it to obtain a perishable crown, but we for an imperishable crown. Therefore I run thus: not with uncertainty. Thus I fight: not as one who beats the air. But **I discipline my body and bring it into subjection**, lest, when I have preached to*

others, I myself should become disqualified." (1 Cor. 9: 24-27)

Anyone striving for mastery in any sport must bring all his other desires and passions into agreement with his pursuit. All his life will be focused on the one vision, and all his energies will serve the grand goal he has set for himself.

As believers, we have the priceless goal of our unspeakable destiny as the Body of Christ, ruling and reigning with Him throughout eternity. There are prizes to be gained. If the athletes of this world sacrifice so much for corruptible crowns that are so fleeting, how much more should the believer practice temperance in the pursuit of the eternal, incorruptible rewards!

With this vision before our hearts, and being persuaded of its glory, we gladly embrace temperance. Our whole lives joyfully come under discipline. Gladly, we cast off the weights that would slow our speed toward the grand prize, sitting with Christ on His throne. We will discover that there are many legitimate things that we really don't need! Temperance is the ability to weigh in the balance what is best, and abstain from the rest. Temperance discerns values, and will sacrifice even lawful things to obtain a higher glory. Mastery comes from temperance.

The Holy Spirit works temperance into us as a fruit of the Spirit. Certainly, we, using our self-will and strength, cannot claim any glory for this miracle. However, by choosing to obey God in all things, we permit the active involvement of the Holy Spirit in our lives. Temperance requires power: the Holy Spirit grants the necessary power. Our wills empowered by the Holy Spirit do not permit our passions to become the controlling influence in our lives, but make them subservient to the purpose of God. The will governs the entire being, and when it is focused on God's purposes, the Holy Spirit fills the entire person.

The fruit of temperance binds all of the fruit together in one beautiful harmony. With temperance, love can be perfectly directed toward God and neighbor!

Thought Questions

1. Why is temperance the final fruit?

2. What happens to power that is not under control?

3. What is the relationship between control and productivity?

4. Peter had to confront teaching that lead to intemperance (2 Pet. 1: 3-11; 2:1-22). Are there parallels today that mistakenly equate liberty to license?

5. Describe how righteousness, temperance, and judgment work together (Acts 24:25).

6. Athletes must exercise temperance in all areas of life to become champions in their sport. Find other examples from life that illustrate this principle. What do these examples teach you about the Christian race?

Chapter Sixteen

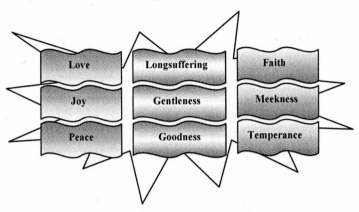

The Key to Unity

The Holy Spirit is the creator of the church. Through the out-poured Spirit, the corporate "people of God" take on shape. The Holy Spirit is responsible not only for the birth of the church, but also for the existence and increase of the church. Therefore life in the Spirit, as evidenced by the fruit of the Spirit, plays center stage in the purposes of God.

The goal of God is the formation of a corporate people for His name, not just a gathering of saved individuals. Three metaphors found in scripture describe the corporate nature of the people of God. With respect to the Father, the church is the family of God. In relation to the Son, the redeemed are the Body of Christ. In terms of the Holy Spirit, the church is the temple of God. How-ever, the realizing agent in all three metaphors is the Holy Spirit.

The key to the existence of the family of God is the Holy Spirit in our midst. The Spirit sent into our hearts causes us to cry out "Abba Father" (Rom. 8:15; Gal. 4:6). The church is built to-

gether as the temple of the Holy Spirit, recognized by the Holy
Spirit's indwelling:

> *"having been built on the foundation of the apostles and
> prophets, Jesus Christ Himself being the chief corner-
> stone, in whom the whole building, being fitted together,
> grows into a holy temple in the Lord, in whom **you also
> are being built together for a dwelling place of God in
> the Spirit.**" (Eph. 2:20-22)*

With the church as the new temple of God, a new covenant is
brought forward with a whole new "order of service" as well.

The concept of the church as the Body of Christ is probably the
most common of the three metaphors to the modern believer.
Again, the reception of the Spirit is what makes this an experienced reality:

> *"For by one Spirit **we were all baptized into one body** -
> whether Jews or Greeks, whether slaves or free - and
> have all been made to drink into one Spirit." (1 Cor.
> 12:13)*

How can believers from so many different backgrounds be
found together in one accord? As we can see from the above
scripture, Paul declares the miracle is the work of the Holy
Spirit.

From this perspective, the eternal purpose of God, centered in
Christ, will provide our understanding of the role of the fruit of
the Spirit as the key to unity:

> *"according to the eternal purpose which He accom-
> plished in Jesus Christ our Lord," (Eph. 3:11)*

From this vantage point, God's eternal purpose for His Son may be summed up in three statements:

o The Father ordained that the Son would have a corporate Body through which to express Himself.

o The Father's intention is that the Son would be the head of this Body, the preeminent One who expresses not only Himself, but also the fullness of the Godhead. Thus the Father and the Holy Spirit are also revealed and expressed throughout the whole universe by the lives of the many sons of God.

o The Son is the reason for all creation. He is the center and gathering point for all things in heaven and earth. All things were created not only by Him, but also for Him.

The purpose of the Father for His Son stretches from eternity to eternity. The current work of God is the preparation and maturation of the Body for its eternal destiny with Christ as His joint-heirs. The building of the Body of Christ now is essential for its participation in Christ's glory that shall be revealed at His appearing. The revelation of this eternal purpose in Christ is taught in the first three chapters of Ephesians. In chapter four, Paul begins to make very practical application. Immediately, we see the fruit of the Spirit mentioned:

*"I, therefore, the prisoner of the Lord, beseech you to walk worthy of the calling with which you were called, with all **lowliness and gentleness, with longsuffering, bearing with one another in love, endeavoring to keep the unity of the Spirit in the bond of peace.** There is one body and one Spirit, just as you were called in one hope of your calling;" (Eph. 4:1-4)*

How is the church edified? How is it built up? How does God prepare the church for its ultimate role as the Bride of Christ, sharing His destiny with Him? To this end, God has given gifts, such as the ministries mentioned in Ephesians 4:11: apostles, prophets, evangelists, pastors and teachers. These are the "craftsmen" that build the house. He also has given the spiritual gifts of First Corinthians 12:8-10 to every member for the Body's profit.

In all of this, however, is the important aspect of the one-another relationships that hold us in fellowship with each other. As glorious as the gifts to the church are, they will all pass away at Christ's appearing. The eternal reality of love remains the foundation of all methods for the edification of the church. Love will not pass away. It is thus the more excellent way, and is the manner in which every method of edification will be effective.

Through the effectual working of every part, God has ordained that the Body would bring increase by the edification of itself in love (Eph. 4:16). Edification takes place when love exists and is practiced between believers. Walking in love is the highest manner in which the Body of Christ will be edified and prepared for its eternal destiny. It is through our relationships that growth will occur in the church (Col. 2:19).

Love will be the eternal nature of the kingdom to which we are called. Therefore love is the training ground in the present, and the means of preparation. To this end, the fruit of the Spirit is practiced in the church as the key to unity; **the fruit makes unity possible and practical**. The fruit of the Spirit, as the expression of the dimensions of love, is the arena where these realities are worked out. How important walking in love toward each other is!

Paul's list of the fruit of the Spirit (Gal. 5:22-23) is found in the context of these one-another relationships. By love, we are to serve one another, and thus fulfill the law. We are not to consume one another, provoke or envy one another. We are to restore each other, and bear one another's burdens (Gal. 5:13-15, 22-23,26; 6:1-2).

There are three clear passages in Paul's writings that directly speak of the fruit of the Spirit's effectiveness in the one-another relationships. They are found in Eph. 4:1-7; Col. 3:11-17; Rom. 12 – 16.

The church at Ephesus was comprised of both Jews and Gentiles, who by natural means could not experience heartfelt unity. Their differences were too great with many irreconcilable disputes among them. However, they were brought together by the common denominator – the Holy Spirit. Eph. 1:11-14 should be understood as "we Jews" and "you Gentiles" were both sealed with the Holy Spirit of promise, which is the earnest of our (both Jews and Gentiles) inheritance:

> *"In Him also we have obtained an inheritance, being predestined according to the purpose of Him who works all things according to the counsel of His will, that we who first trusted in Christ should be to the praise of His glory. In Him you also trusted, after you heard the word of truth, the gospel of your salvation; in whom also, having believed,* **you were sealed with the Holy Spirit of promise,** *who is the guarantee of our inheritance until the redemption of the purchased possession, to the praise of His glory." (Eph. 1:11- 14)*

Ephesians 2:18-22 also states that the Holy Spirit is the unifying factor for both Jews and Gentiles.

Since the Holy has produced a fellowship and kinship among them, only life in the Spirit will maintain them in such relationships. While they cannot produce unity, their experience in the Holy Spirit does: *"endeavoring to keep the **unity of the Spirit** in the bond of peace." (Eph. 4:3)* They were together in one body because there is only one Spirit (Eph. 4:4). Therefore it was the fruit of the Spirit in their lives that harmonized them as the Body of Christ in the face of potential arguments. They walked worthy of the vocation wherewith they were called by practicing all lowliness and meekness, with longsuffering, forbearing one another in love, and endeavoring to keep the unity of the Spirit in the bond of peace (Eph. 4:1-3). Notice the emphasis on meekness, longsuffering, and peace in this passage. These are all fruit of the Spirit that make unity possible!

By reading Colossians 3:11-17, you will discover that Paul gave similar advice to the Colossians and the Ephesians. From the natural point of view, there was great potential for strife and division, but Christ was all and in all. As the elect of God, they were to put on tender mercies, kindness, humbleness of mind, meekness, longsuffering, forbearing one another and forgiving one another. If there were quarrels (and we can be sure there were), they were to forgive as Christ had forgiven each of them, and to put on love above all things, for love is the bond of perfection. The peace of God was to rule in their hearts, for they were called into one body. It was the experience in, and the anointing of the Holy Spirit that made this possible. Together they could be thankful, teach and admonish each other, and sing psalms and hymns and spiritual songs with grace in their hearts to the Lord. As in the passage in Ephesians, fruit of the Spirit such as gentleness, meekness, longsuffering, love, and peace brought unity among a very diverse group of people.

The same truth is brought forth in the epistle to the Romans.
This book begins with a discussion of the sinful state of both
Jews and Gentiles, and progresses to its climax in Chapter 12,
describing the Body of Christ.

> *"I beseech you therefore, brethren, by the mercies of*
> *God, that you present your bodies a living sacrifice,*
> *holy, acceptable to God, which is your reasonable ser-*
> *vice. And do not be conformed to this world, but be*
> *transformed **by the renewing of your mind, that you***
> ***may prove what is that good and acceptable and perfect***
> ***will of God." (Rom. 12:1-2)***

We are to give ourselves to the Lord that we may prove what is
the good, acceptable, and perfect will of God. Before we can
envision the perfect will of God, our minds need to be renewed.
The fruit of the Spirit must be developed within us. Then, we
will function successfully as diverse members of the Body of
Christ. After the doctrine of salvation was set forth in the first
chapters, Paul explained the will and purpose of God: Christ is
the firstborn among many brethren (Rom. 8:28-30).

The many brethren form the Body of Christ. Once again, Jews
and Gentiles are in the same Body. Paul, in his presentation of
redemption throughout the epistle, has been dealing with some
of the many sharp differences between Jews and Gentiles, such
as issues over the law. How is it that Jews who had received the
law were on the same footing as the Gentiles who had no law?
This kind of question revealed some of the difficulties these
members might have had with one another.

After the great climax is reached in Chapter 12, revealing the
will of God as the emergence of the Body of Christ, the remainder of the letter deals with the practical. References to the fruit

of the Spirit abound, for only the Spirit-filled life can overcome such natural differences.

Love, joy, and peace are the first to be mentioned. Love is to be without hypocrisy (12:9), and they are to be kindly affectionate to one another with brotherly love (12:10). They are to rejoice in hope (12:12). As much as possible, they are to be in peace with all men (12:18). They are admonished not to be overcome by evil, but overcome evil with good (12:21). Love is the key to unity, and fulfills all the law's requirements (13:8-10).

In Chapter 14, Paul deals with specific situations that could cause contention between Jews and Gentiles: acceptable foods, and days to set aside to the Lord. Paul is more concerned with their attitudes than he is with the solutions. They are not to cause each other to stumble, but they are admonished to edify each other. They are to walk in love (14:15), for the kingdom of God is not wrapped up in meat and drink, but it does consist of the fruit of the Spirit, such as peace and joy (14:17). Believers are to follow after things that make for peace (14:19).

Paul continues his exhortation in Chapter 15, emphasizing goodness (15:2,14) and that the God of hope will fill them all with joy and peace (15:13). He beseeches them to pray because of the love of the Spirit (15:30) that he might visit them with joy (15:32). He terminates this long exhortation to unity by calling God the God of peace (15:33).

To end this letter, Paul greets many people by name (16:1-16). Paul himself was a living example of warm and close fellowship with other believers. He speaks of them with affectionate terms, thanking each of them personally.

*"Now I urge you, brethren, **note those who cause divisions and offenses, contrary to the doctrine which you learned, and avoid them.** For those who are such do not serve our Lord Jesus Christ, but their own belly, and by smooth words and flattering speech deceive the hearts of the simple. For your obedience has become known to all. Therefore I am glad on your behalf; but I want you to be wise in what is good, and simple concerning evil. And the God of peace will crush Satan under your feet shortly. The grace of our Lord Jesus Christ be with you. Amen." (Rom. 16:17-20)*

Paul warned the Romans that there would be some who act contrary to the fruit of the Spirit and would cause divisions (16:17-18). To counter this, he encouraged them to embrace goodness (16:19). As he completed the epistle, he once more referred to God as the God of peace (16:20).

It is God's will for members of the church to relate to one another by life in the Spirit. The fruit of the Spirit is seen as the key to unity in the midst of background diversities. The church is the arena where eternal principles of life and truth are experientially learned and developed, as members relate one to another. All true doctrine declares love to be an absolutely essential ingredient of Christian life; and thus the church is edified and prepared for its glorious destiny.

Thought Questions

1. According to this chapter, what is the goal of God?

2. What three metaphors does Paul use to describe the corporate people of God? How is the Holy Spirit the crucial ingredient causing each metaphor to function?

3. What is God's current work?

4. What is the manner in which every method of edification is most effective?

5. How can people from various backgrounds, such as Jews and Gentiles, come together in unity? Explain your answer.

6. Give a discussion relating fruit and unity, using the following scriptures: Eph. 4:1-7; Col. 3:11-17; Rom. 12-16.

Chapter 17

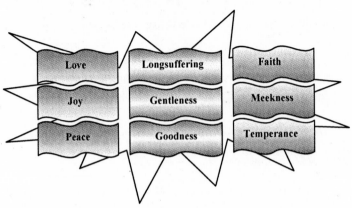

In Summary

The fruit of the Spirit produces temperance (self-control), enabling us to love God and neighbor. Love is the sum of all the fruit, and temperance binds it together in one beautiful harmony. Paul prayed for the Philippians that they would be filled with the fruit of righteousness (Phi. 1:11). The dealings of the Lord bring about the peaceable fruit of righteousness (Heb. 12:11).

God is love (1 John 4:8), and His character and nature is reproduced in the Spirit-filled believer. The Lord is merciful and gracious, longsuffering and abundant in goodness and truth, keeps mercy for thousands, and forgives unrighteous acts (wickedness) and sin (Ex. 34:6-7). The nature of God is to love, and to be a blessing to all He meets. We are able to walk in goodness toward others at all times because that is the inherent nature of love. A grain of wheat can only produce wheat; love only knows how to love, for that is its nature. As assuredly as sparks fly upward and gravity pulls downward at all times, the fruit of love can do nothing but good to its neighbor. The fruit of love, as expressed in the fruit of the Spirit, desires to overcome evil and hatred with its blessings. All obstacles merely make the manifestation of the fruit of love more triumphant.

How does the believer move into a lifestyle in which love is the norm? Truly self-effort cannot achieve the metamorphosis. This magnificent character change occurs as Christ is formed in us:

> *"My little children, for whom I labor in birth again **until Christ is formed in you**." (Gal. 4:19)*

> *"I have been crucified with Christ; it is no longer I who live, **but Christ lives in me**; and the life which I now live in the flesh I live by faith in the Son of God, who loved me and gave Himself for me." (Gal. 2:20)*

> *"But **we all**, with unveiled face, beholding as in a mirror the glory of the Lord, **are being transformed into the same image from glory to glory**, just as by the Spirit of the Lord." (2 Cor. 3:18)*

The New Testament declares that a believer has a new heart. God has taken away the stony heart and has given instead a fleshly heart. Upon that new heart He writes His laws. This is done with the pen of the Holy Spirit (Jer. 31:31-34; Ezek. 36:26-27). The Old Testament failed because the Spirit was not given; the New Testament succeeds because of the Holy Spirit's presence in our lives. Paul said:

> *"clearly **you are an epistle of Christ**, ministered by us, written not with ink but by the Spirit of the living God, not on tablets of stone but **on tablets of flesh, that is, of the heart**." (2 Cor. 3:3)*

Paul's exhortation in Romans 12:1-2 shows us the way to the fruit of the Spirit as exemplified through Chapters 12–16. We have a part; God has a part. Our part as believers is to present our bodies as living sacrifices. That is consecration, and it involves saying no to that which is wrong (Rom. 6:13). We are to set our wills to agree with the will of God. Consecration also means to give up all things to the Lord, and be devoted to Him in all areas of our lives.

God's part is to do the work of renewal as we set our wills to obey Him. The Holy Spirit empowers us to accomplish what the flesh cannot, changing us from within both to will and to do His good pleasure (Phil. 2:13). The Holy Spirit does the work of renewal (Tit. 3:5). God writes His laws upon our hearts and minds (Heb. 8:8-12). The Holy Spirit etches the law of the Spirit of life upon the tables of our hearts. This law produces the disposition of love as the normal state of being. **Love, the nature of God Himself, only knows how to bless, edify, and encourage.**

This wonderful work of the Holy Spirit provides a powerful witness to the world, for as we fulfill the new command to love one another, all men will know that we are Christ's disciples (John 13:34-35).

Against such fruit as love, joy, peace, longsuffering, gentleness, goodness, faith, meekness, and temperance, there is no law. The fruit of the Spirit powerfully demonstrates righteousness.

Thought Questions

1. What is the nature of love? What does it seek to do?

2. God has His part in the work of renewal. What is the believer's part?

3. Give a brief overview of how the fruit of the Spirit demonstrates righteousness.

Contact Eugene and Darla Smith,
to inquire about
Freedom Alive Ministries,
and other teaching and music materials.

Please visit their website:

www.freedomalive.ca

Printed in the United States
3462